Paying Back

Twenty Years of Community Service

Paying Back

Twenty Years of Community Service

Edited by

Dick Whitfield and David Scott

With a Foreword by
The Rt Hon Lord Taylor of Gosforth PC,
Lord Chief Justice

WATERSIDE PRESS

Paying Back
Twenty Years of Community Service

Edited by Dick Whitfield and David Scott

Published 1993 by
WATERSIDE PRESS
Domum Road,
Winchester SO23 9NN

Book orders
Waterside Press
Freepost
Winchester SO23 9BR
Telephone or Fax 0962 855567

ISBN Paperback 1 872870 13 9

1735148

Printing and binding Antony Rowe Ltd, Chippenham

Contributors

JOHN CRAWFORTH is currently Deputy Chief Probation Officer for Lancashire. He began his career in the Probation Service in 1974 in Greater Manchester and in the early 1980s led a large community service team serving the cities of Manchester and Salford. Later, as an Assistant Chief Probation Officer, he had a county-wide responsibility for community service. He has always taken a keen interest in wider criminal justice issues and holds a Master of Philosophy degree in Criminology from the University of Cambridge.

LAWRENCE FRAYNE has been Chief Probation Officer in Wiltshire since 1974. He started as a probation officer in Bristol in 1962 and was Assistant Principal Probation Officer in Devon from 1970 to 1974. For five crucial years from 1985 to 1990 he also chaired the ACOP Community Service Committee.

JEAN HINE is Research and Information Officer with Derbyshire Probation Service. She has worked as a researcher within the probation service since 1974, during which time she has regularly undertaken evaluation of community service in all its aspects. She undertook the National Study of Community Service (a major Home Office sponsored research project) for the University of Birmingham from 1980 to 1990.

IAN McNAIR is Assistant Chief Probation Officer in the West Midlands Probation Service, currently with responsibility for training. After joining the Probation Service in Nottinghamshire in 1972 he later became a senior probation officer in Gloucestershire and was Community Service Organiser for that county. He later took lead responsibility for community service in the West Midlands as part of his work as Assistant Chief Probation Officer there. His experience includes an extended vocational visit to the Los Angeles area.

BOB MORRIS is the Assistant Under Secretary of State in the Home Office responsible for the Criminal Justice and Constitutional Department. This includes Her Majesty's Inspectorate of Probation and the Probation Services Division (C6). He has worked in the Home Office since 1961, covering all but one (Children's Department) of the criminal justice functions for which the Home Office has in his time had responsibility.

MARK OLDFIELD is Research and Information Officer for Kent Probation Service. His research career began in the information section of an NHS Family Practitioner Committee. He then spent six years in the Research Unit of Sheffield Social Services Department before moving to London to take up the post of assistant research officer with Middlesex Probation Service, joining Kent in 1989.

ANDREW RUTHERFORD is a Reader in Law at Southampton University. From 1962 to 1973 he was an Assistant and Deputy Governor in the prison service. Since 1984 he has been Chairman of the Howard League for Penal Reform. He is the author of *Prisons and the Process of Justice* (1986), *Growing out of Crime: The New Era* (1992) and *Criminal Justice and the Pursuit of Decency* (1993).

DAVID SCOTT is the Chief Probation Officer for West Sussex. He gained his degree in Behavioural Science at the University of Aston in Birmingham and his CQSW at the University of Bristol. After working as a probation officer, he spent four years with Hampshire Probation Service as Training Senior in the Home Office Training Unit. He is currently in the final year of an MBA with the Open University.

DICK WHITFIELD is Chief Probation Officer for Kent and until recently chaired the Community Service Committee of the Association of Chief Officers of Probation. He is vice-chair of the Howard League for Penal Reform and edited *The State of the Prisons—200 years on* (1991).

JOE WOODS has been the Senior Probation Officer responsible for managing community service throughout Derbyshire for the last three years. During 1980/81 he was involved in a job exchange with the probation service in Ontario, Canada where he organised community service as a condition of a supervision order. He also has experience of the probation service in both Australia and New Zealand.

Royalties

All royalties from the sale of this book have been donated by the authors to the following two charitable funds:

Probation Educational and Research Trust
which promotes research and study within the probation service.

The Edridge Fund
of the National Association of Probation Officers, which gives financial help to those in need.

Paying Back
Twenty Years of Community Service

Contents

Contents (continued)

WATERSIDE PRESS
Winchester

Foreword

The Rt. Hon. LORD TAYLOR OF GOSFORTH PC, Lord Chief Justice

Since its introduction in 1973, the community service order has grown to be one of the most durable and effective sentencing options available to the court when dealing with offenders for whom neither a custodial sentence nor a fine would be appropriate. In 1992, 43,000 community service orders were made: 10% of the total of all sentences and 13% of those made by the Crown Court.

This collection of essays is therefore a timely contribution to our criminology. Starting with the dual purposes of the order, both to provide a means of re-integrating criminals into society through positive and demanding unpaid work, and at the same time to make reparation to the community itself, the contributors examine key aspects of the history, practice and objectives of the community service order from a number of standpoints. Analogies from other jurisdictions are discussed, as are the important changes affected by the Criminal Justice Act 1991.

A greater understanding of the way community service orders are used, and how they operate in practice, will be of benefit not only to lawyers, probation officers and other practitioners, but also to all those with an interest in the development of our criminal law.

Taylor CJ

12

Chapter 1 Introduction

Bob Morris

Community service orders (CSOs), which require an offender to perform unpaid work in the community, were introduced in 1973, and in the 20 years since then they have become an important part of the sentencing framework. The probation service's success with the innovation took it into new fields which undoubtedly encouraged Parliament to agree to a significant enhancement of the service's role in the criminal justice system.

Since the implementation of the Criminal Justice Act 1991 in October 1992 an increased emphasis has been placed on the use of community sentences such as CSOs for more serious offences and, as the perception of community sentences as constituting punishment in the community has grown, the use of community service has increased.

In 1992 43,000 orders were commenced, the highest total ever.

History of community service in the criminal justice system

The 1970 report of the Advisory Council on the Penal System—'Non Custodial and Semi-Custodial Penalties' (the Wootton Report)—noted a widespread recognition among sentencers that a new non-custodial penalty was required, and suggested that offenders should be required to engage in unpaid service to the community. The intention behind the proposals was that the sentence would be punitive in that the offender would be deprived of leisure time. However, it was hoped that constructive activity in the community might also result in a changed outlook on the part of the offender.

Community service was introduced in England and Wales by the Criminal Justice Act 1972, implemented on 1 January 1973, starting with experimental schemes in six probation areas. Evaluation of these schemes showed the CSO to be viable and further schemes were developed from 1975 onwards and by March 1979 arrangements were in place in the final area, Dyfed.

Under the 1972 Act community service (CS) was available to the courts for an offender aged 17 or over convicted of an imprisonable offence, who could be required to perform between 40 to 240 hours work. The Criminal Justice Act 1982 extended CS to 16 year olds, with the upper limit reduced to 120 hours for this age group.

Whilst the 1972 Act introduced CS as an alternative to custody, the practical outcome was different. The effect of subsequent Court of Appeal rulings was that, although longer CSOs (of around 150 hours or more) could be made where custody would otherwise have been the outcome, shorter CSOs could be made as alternatives to *other* non-custodial penalties.

By 1976 the number of orders commenced had risen to 8,740, and by 1979 to

15,720. This rise continued to a peak of 37,560 in 1985. There followed a slight decline until 1989 when, prompted by concern about the trend, the Home Office introduced National Standards for community service orders—the first ever for any probation service activity. Drawn up after consultation with the probation service, sentencers and others, the standards were intended to contribute towards winning the confidence of the courts by setting requirements for all area probation services and thereby established clear expectations for others regarding good practice. Particular issues covered in the standards included arrangements for dealing with breaches of orders. Practice had varied widely and inconsistencies were leading to some loss of confidence among sentencers concerned about whether CSOs were being enforced properly. Following the introduction of National Standards the decline in new orders was reversed and since 1989 there has been a steady annual growth in demand.

Punishment in the community
The concept of punishment in the community was developed in the 1988 Green Paper 'Punishment, Custody and the Community', and restated in the 1990 White Paper 'Crime, Justice and Protecting the Public'. The main theme was a recognition, first, of the potentially damaging effects of custody (summed up in the phrase 'prison can be an expensive way of making bad people worse') and, second, that community sentences can be effective as punishment through the restriction on liberty that they involve. These themes led to the idea that, for many less serious offenders, a community sentence could be both more appropriate and more effective. The new sentencing arrangements introduced by the Criminal Justice Act 1991 are based on a development of these ideas to restrict the use of custody to the most serious cases, placing the emphasis on punishment in the community in less serious cases.

The Criminal Justice Act 1991
The Criminal Justice Act 1991 made significant changes to the sentencing framework in England and Wales and placed increased emphasis on the use of community sentences. Under the new framework a *custodial* sentence may be made only when the court is satisfied that the offence is so serious that no other sentence can be justified, or when such a sentence is necessary to protect the public from serious harm from the offender. A *community* sentence may be passed when the offence is serious enough to justify this restriction of liberty; and the sentence falls to be chosen from the range of community sentences available as the one most suitable for the needs of the offender, commensurate with the seriousness of the offence. For less serious offences the courts retain discharges, fines and compensation orders.

Effects on CSOs
Under the Act community service became available to the courts for an offender aged 16 or over convicted of an offence 'serious enough' to warrant such a sentence. Another change was the introduction of the combination order, combining a probation order of one to three years with a CSO of 40 to 100 hours. The idea of such a combination had first been mentioned in the Wootton report, *supra*, which suggested that, whilst for some offenders a community

14

service order alone would be appropriate, for others it would be more suitable to make a probation order with an additional requirement to perform community service.

A revised version of the 1989 community service National Standard was included in 'National Standards for the Supervision of Offenders in the Community' which was produced to coincide with the October 1992 implementation of the 1991 Act. These Standards, produced after extensive and detailed consultation with probation practitioners and managers, set minimum standards for good practice. They covered all areas of probation service work with offenders including the preparation of pre-sentence reports for the courts, supervision of offenders under probation or supervision orders, community service and combination orders, pre-release and post-release supervision of offenders serving custodial sentences, and the management of approved hostels. The Standards set requirements for the probation service and expectations for others regarding the level and type of supervision which should be given, and are an effective tool for management as well as for service delivery. By setting out clearly the type of supervision provided the standards contribute to a wider awareness and confidence on the part of sentencers and the public in the work of the probation service, and counter a popular but erroneous belief that prison is the only real punishment.

Objectives of community service orders
National standards for the supervision of offenders in the community state that:

'The main purpose of a CSO is to reintegrate the offender into the community through:
      —positive and demanding unpaid work, and
      —reparation to the community'

Work placements arranged for offenders serving CSOs should be demanding, of benefit to the community, and should also, wherever possible, be personally fulfilling for offenders and designed to secure public support for the supervision of offenders in the community.

The work can involve reparation directed to a greater or lesser degree to victims, for example fitting security locks in the homes of vulnerable people, but work performed under a CSO will usually be of more general benefit to the community. The type of work depends very much on the projects in operation in the local area in question, but the range is huge; from clearing canals or footpaths to providing care and assistance for elderly people or those with disabilities. There are many examples of projects undertaken by community service teams, for example the conversion of two old shops into a community centre for a local Bangladeshi community, a weekly shopping trip for disabled people who would otherwise be housebound, a project to collect and renovate unwanted furniture which is then given to needy families, and many more equally impressive initiatives.

When planning the provision of work placements it is important to see the work from the viewpoint of the offender, for what might seem a very simple requirement from the viewpoint of someone used to regular work and conformity may be very different when viewed from that of an offender. Many offenders have a very chaotic lifestyle; often they are either unemployed or working for short spells as casual labour, so that the discipline required to report regularly, on time, for community work may represent a significant challenge in itself. Other offenders may find communication difficult and working in a team on a group project may represent a significant challenge, and also help them to develop basic social skills. Work involving an aspect of caring and of interaction with the recipients of that care—for example helping at day centres for elderly people—can also be very demanding for offenders with poorly developed social skills.

Whilst the primary intention of community service is punitive, it is important to remember that this aim is largely achieved through the loss of leisure time and the work should not of itself be the punishment; the aim is for the offender to complete the order successfully and this is most likely to be achieved where the work, whilst demanding, is positive and can give the offender a sense of achievement. Setting an offender up to fail by providing boring and demeaning work placements would be counterproductive.

Many offenders have little confidence or self-esteem; they frequently have few skills or qualifications, and part of the appeal of offending may be a sense of achievement. Community service provides an opportunity for constructive and rewarding activities which may replace the 'buzz' of offending. Working in a team to produce a concrete and visible result which is of benefit to those seen to be less fortunate—for example the ill or the elderly—can give a sense of achievement and confidence; the knowledge that a housebound elderly person is relying on his help to go shopping may give an offender a sense of responsibility for someone other than himself.

The result of carefully chosen and managed community service can be a change in attitude on the part of the offender. The overall aim is that having been given a sense of achievement, possibly having learned or improved skills, and having built working relationships with the other members of the group or with the recipients of his work the offender will be less likely to reoffend and more likely to have found constructive ways of occupying free time. Many people continue with voluntary work at projects where they performed community service, enjoying the satisfaction of helping others and the friendship of the people they are helping.

Public image of community service

At a time of increased public concern about the growth in reported crime it is important that the probation service should be able to demonstrate publicly the effectiveness and value of this work. National Standards are a useful tool in reinforcing the point that community sentences are not a soft option for offenders who would otherwise be in prison, but are tough and demanding penalties which make real demands on offenders and which are taken seriously by the courts and by the probation service.

By its nature, community service offers a chance for the probation service to raise public awareness of the good work being done with offenders in the community. Some of the work performed by community service teams makes a highly visible contribution to improving the local environment, and identifying an impressive project as having been performed by CS workers can provide an effective way of publicising the work of the service.

The future of community service
In the 20 years since its introduction, community service has developed to become one of the central planks of the sentencing framework. Development is a constant process and will doubtless continue, so the question is where should community service go from here?

The wide range of community sentences available to the courts, of which CS is just one, means that the courts must choose which sentence is the most suitable for the individual offender. In advising the court, through a pre-sentence report, about possible sentences the probation service has an important influence, but the decision on sentencing remains with the court and it is therefore essential that the courts are fully informed about the merits of all available options. There is a balance to be achieved between probation, community service and combination orders; as all those involved in the criminal justice system become increasingly familiar with the sentencing provisions of the 1991 Act and subsequently announced refinements, this balance should become clearer. If the rise in the use of community service continues it will be necessary for the allocation of resources between the various activities of the probation service to be reviewed to enable the service to give full effect to the courts sentencing decisions. Thought will also need to be given to the organisation of community service within area probation services. Community service can become 'semi-detached' from the mainstream probation practice. Increasingly, the development of the combination order will require management to consider how the integration of two supervision activities should be matched to ensure continuity and consistency of approach.

The CSO is an undoubted success, and is here to stay, but it will continue to require constant attention and development to be sure of retaining the support of sentencers in the developed sentencing framework of punishment in the community which remains at the heart of the 1991 Act. The probation service rose to the initial challenge of its introduction and must be counted on to continue its constant renewal by the intelligent and active engagement of new generations of probation service members. Their continued ability to achieve this will do much to influence the regard in which the service is held and the position it holds in the criminal justice system as a whole.

Chapter 2 The History of Change

Lawrence Frayne

The starting point

'A court order which deprived an offender of his leisure and required him to undertake tasks for the community would necessarily be felt to have a punitive element. What attracts us, however, is the opportunity which it could give for constructive activity in the form of personal service to the community, and the possibility of a changed outlook on the part of the offender. We would hope that offenders required to perform community service would come to see it in this light, and not as wholly negative and punitive.' (Report of the Sub-Committee on Non-Custodial and Semi-Custodial Penalties, para 34).

The early history of events leading to the introduction of community service by offenders stretched across the political spectrum both in time and attitudes. The work of the sub-committee of the Advisory Council on the Penal System under Baroness Wootton (1) began as a result of a request by the Rt Hon Roy Jenkins, a Labour Home Secretary, but was presented to the Rt Hon Reginald Maudling, a Conservative. The process started in November 1966, the report was sent to the Home Secretary in June 1970 and the resulting Criminal Justice Bill was debated during 1972, leading to the Criminal Justice Act 1972, with the Powers of Criminal Courts Act 1973 following a year later. This brought the new penalty into being.

Baroness Wootton's sub-committee foresaw many of the issues which were to be reflected in Parliamentary debate and then amongst practitioners in the probation service. These included punishment versus reform, care versus control, short time-span to encourage success versus longer time to widen the sentencing scope.

In one respect the sub-committee promoted an idealistic approach which soon proved unrealistic in practice. It was thought that there were numerous voluntary organisations which would welcome offenders to work with them and it was felt that shared enterprise would lead to shared values. Some of this belief has informed the resulting arrangements and has been incorporated into most schemes but the number of worker/offenders soon outnumbered the volunteer workers. Although it was suggested that given time, more voluntary groups could be formed it was soon impossible to avoid the organisation of projects entirely by the probation service.

One guiding principle was put forward by the Wootton Committee which has usually been observed both on practical grounds and for reasons which should guide the philosophy of the proposals. This was spelt out in the following terms (para 41):

'We are particularly anxious to avoid decisions which might smack of gimmickry and so undermine public confidence. The scheme that we have in mind therefore, is intended, not to compel the offender to undergo some form of penance directly related to his offence, which would have only a limited application, but to require him to perform service of value to the community or to those in need.'

This clear statement has enabled the organisers of projects to resist schemes with an element of humiliation or of punishment for its own sake even though these have often been advocated. The practical value of the statement was tested early in one scheme in which workers were required to move paper and other debris which blew regularly from a rubbish tip against a fence at the side of a main railway line. The work was pointless since, in the absence of good management of the tip, more debris accumulated as quickly as it was cleared. It caused some amusement to passengers but workers soon refused to work on this project.

In spite of the painstaking way in which the committee had thought through and examined their own proposals, it was still thought wise to test them out in practice before finally incorporating them in legislation. This proved impossible because, at that time, a probation order was an alternative to a sentence and a condition to undertake work (which was the way in which it was thought to be feasible) was considered to be a sentence. However, it was proposed that even after legislation had made community service orders possible, there should be pilot schemes which might develop differing characteristics, and which could be studied before a nationwide spread was undertaken.

The sub-committee considered possible alternatives for the organisation of community service by offenders and reached the conclusion that it should be the responsibility of the probation service. This service already had a national network, was involved with work with offenders and already operated in and with courts. The proposal was both practical and economic.

These recommendations were accepted by the government and were incorporated into a Bill to be steered through the Commons by the Minister of State at the Home Office, Mark Carlisle.

The Commons debates
These were marked by much goodwill and an obvious wish on all sides to produce a workable and humane scheme. Questions raised ranged from whether the order was an alternative to custody to whether it should be used for direct reparation to the injured party. Should the offender give consent or be ordered to work? Should the materials needed for the work be paid for from public funds? Would the work be confined to that which would not be done by paid labour? How would the problems of insurance be dealt with? Would the order be available for fine default? Would the work be genuinely of value to the community? Why was the maximum number of hours 240 instead of 120 as recommended? Would the workers be seen as in a 'chain gang'? Would the work

be seen as punitive or reformative? These and many more issues were explored in a series of debates.

Mark Carlisle dealt as best he could with these matters. It was hoped that community service 'will help to keep out of prison some people who would now go there'; 'it deprives a man of his free time and requires him to do something for society'; the offender must consent or the order to work would be in breach of the European Convention on Human Rights; the Trade Union Conference had resolved to work to reduce the prison population and could be expected to support this measure; 240 hours had been chosen to given encouragement to the consideration that community service was a genuine alternative to a prison sentence.

However, at the end of the discussion it was made clear that this was a large measure; an innovation and a new step for the probation service and the courts. In these circumstances it was accepted that there would need to be a trial period in five areas. These would be Nottinghamshire, Durham, Kent, Inner London and South West Lancashire. They were chosen because of the variety they offered and the introduction of the schemes would be monitored by the Home Office Research Unit so that guidance on good practice could be clearly available and relevant before community service by offenders spread nationwide.

The pilot projects
With a rising number of prisoners and considerable unrest within the prisons no time was lost in testing the viability of community service by offenders. Senior probation officers were appointed for each of the project areas, including Shropshire (which was added to the original five) and given three months in which to prepare. All the areas were then given permission to start from 1 January 1973. The Home Office monitoring was to last for two years. The three months for preparation was woefully inadequate but it did mean that on one hand there was a sense of excited anticipation and on the other there was a need to face quickly the doubts, anxieties and obstructiveness which came from various sources. The Wootton Committee and the legislators expected that there would be close co-operation, consultation and partnership with a wide variety of voluntary and statutory agencies. Fears were expressed that the work undertaken would eat into a shrinking job market for paid workers and consultation was expected with trade unions. There was considerable anxiety within the probation service that the necessary strong element of control and imposed discipline would change the nature and values of the service. The courts needed to be convinced that this was a sentence which could be trusted to give safe and constructive supervision to offenders who might otherwise go to prison.

To help in tackling all these issues Community Service Committees were formed by Probation Committees to operate within a probation framework but having more autonomy than a normal sub-committee and usually having control of its own budget. It came to be accepted practice to co-opt on to these committees a prominent member of a Trade Union to allay fears that work would be sought which would normally be done by paid workers.

Not surprisingly, the background of the senior probation officers influenced the way the schemes developed. Those with some experience and training in

20

community work put great emphasis on the service to the community, feeling that punishment was an inevitable reality and rehabilitation would be a desirable and likely by-product if the service to the community was obviously worthwhile. Others put more emphasis on the organising of a viable, economic and accountable scheme in which emphasis was on discipline and leaned more towards a view that regularity in work was not only of value for its own sake but also enabled the offender to make some recompense to society for the harm caused by his or her offending.

The cost of the scheme in the pilot areas was to be borne 100% by the Home Office but forecasting the financial implications was, inevitably, guesswork. Some of the most gifted of the original senior probation officers had flair, imagination, drive and considerable qualities of leadership but the more routine attributes which lead to good systems of budgetary control, administration and collection of data for monitoring were less in evidence and subsequently led to considerable difficulty when the scheme was to go nationwide.

However, the fact that the money was provided by the Home Office was a key factor in getting the experiments off to a rapid start. The organisers did not need to argue the case for resources against the background of demands already being faced by area probation services for other developments.

In three of the areas the organisers sought to achieve an understanding with the workers that there were a number of jobs to be done in differing settings and requiring matching skills or at least a willingness to learn. The belief behind this was that work for the community needed some commitment both in regularity and quality; this was most likely to be achieved if the offender felt treated with respect and that his/her co-operation was sought. In Nottingham this was made obvious in two ways. In the first case it was made clear in the agreed aims of the scheme:

1 Community service should be a worthwhile experience for the offender.
2 Community service should offer tangible benefits to the community or a section of the community.
3 Community service should take place in or near a person's locality unless the subject is keen to pursue an activity outside his or her area such as nature preservation, archaeological digs etc.
4 Community service should offer the participant an opportunity to continue service after the expiration of the order.

The second way in which respect was shown to the offender by one of the organisers, and co-operation sought, was established at the very beginning with the question 'What do you think you have to offer?'

The Wootton Committee had sought advice from voluntary organisations when addressing the issues of supply of work and had 'been assured that there is an abundance of opportunity for community service both in work with or for individuals and in constructional projects.' When the organisers started, however, the work and the voluntary organisations were not always apparent and in Nottingham over seventy organisations were contacted in the three months before the first order was made. In addition local authorities and hospital administrations were approached and brought a very mixed response. All needed

21

quite a lot of re-assurance that selection would be rigorously controlled and supervision not left entirely to them. Local authority chief officers and their deputies needed to be certain that they were acting within the policies set by elected members and so council committees had to be addressed. All of this brought members of the probation service into the limelight in a way which was quite unfamiliar, but public interest was being aroused and some of the organisers became very public figures, sometimes nationally known. Within a year the tide began to turn and the new community service units were being approached by organisations for help, more in line with the expectations of the Wootton Committee.

The possibility of considerable organisational problems had been noted by the Wootton Committee as a likely result of uneven flow of workers with necessary skills for the work on offer. This was compounded by the equally uneven provision of work by some voluntary organisations which tended to be more active in the summer. Systematic controls to ensure that workers 'did not slack', were in the right place at the right time, that they were adequately supervised, performing well and producing work of adequate quality had now to be built into schemes. Courts had to be alerted to the issues surrounding failures of one kind or another and the necessary action to enforce breaches of the orders. But this was not all that had to be done with courts. The law relating to community service orders was quite straightforward and not considered likely to cause many problems but one matter emerged from the beginning. It concerned the place of a community service order on the sentencing 'tariff'. Section 15(1) Criminal Justice Act 1972 stated:

'Where a person who has attained the age of 17 is convicted of an offence punishable with imprisonment, the court . . . may instead of dealing with him in any other way . . . make an order (in this Act referred to as a Community Service Order).'

In some pilot areas it was suggested very firmly that this implied that these orders should only be used as an alternative to a prison sentence and by and large this was accepted by the courts in those areas. In other places the view was expressed that since the statute did not specifically state that it was an alternative, it left it open to be used as the court saw fit. It led to a friendly controversy which was to run and run and was only to be ended with the Criminal Justice Act 1991 which replaced the concept of alternatives to prison with proportionality (just deserts).

Other discussions then developed about what could be considered 'a short prison sentence' and how many hours would be equivalent to a month's imprisonment. This was not finally resolved in the trial period but in Nottingham it was taken as a rough guide that 120 hours equated with a 6 month prison sentence (2) and this was to provide a benchmark as the community service provision subsequently spread to other areas. More practical problems for sentencers had to be discussed when consideration had to be given to what recommendations should be made when people in breach of the order returned to court.

Faced with a new sentence and the possibility of making orders for community service it was not surprising that magistrates and judges took a keen interest in the work proposed. The organisers found themselves at the centre of some heated discussions between those who felt the work should be punishing and those more interested in reparation and rehabilitation who wanted it to provide a positive experience with the hope that it would expand both the abilities and the understanding of the offenders when they were faced with people in great need. The debates usually led to balanced conclusions and considerable support for the organisers but they demonstrated how vitally important such discussions were and led to a development which had not been entirely foreseen. The first organisers rapidly became the 'experts' in this new field and were in great demand to advertise the scheme and offer advice as the time drew near for likely expansion nationwide. To some extent the public imagination had been caught and the earlier discussions amongst sentencers were repeated in more open debate in and with the media. The early experiences of community service workers were eagerly awaited.

In the meantime all was not plain sailing for community service staff with their colleagues in the probation service. Consent was seen as 'Hobson's choice', the staffing levels in community service did not allow for practical or emotional problems to be adequately addressed and the whole concept of strict imposed discipline ran counter to some officers' social work ideals. However, there was for many an interesting challenge because social work training up to that point had been based largely on the premise that treatment for all sorts of difficulties could best emerge from a personal but professional relationship between offender and officer. In this context problems could be identified, shared and (hopefully) solved. The emphasis was on tackling the negative and difficult issues. Community service offered a chance to look at the offenders in quite a different way based on John Harding's question in Nottingham, 'What do you think you have to offer?'

This more positive way of looking at offenders, which allowed for recognition of abilities and released their compassion, thoughtfulness and commitment to people in need of help, expanded the social work methods used in the probation service. It was not entirely new but it was complementary to the most widely held view of social casework at the time, ie that it was a problem solving process. The service was able to use the skills and experience of a wide variety of people in voluntary agencies and has employed sessional supervisors to expand the knowledge and self confidence of many offenders who previously took to crime out of boredom and frustration.

The service was widening its basis of work with offenders but this change, institutionalised as it was by the separate Community Service Committees and the 100% Home Office funding, led to much suspicion. There was a danger that the new units could develop quite a separate existence and the organisers had to make considerable efforts to avoid this. One practical way of doing so was to make arrangements with field team officers to deal with emotional, family or practical problems on a voluntary basis. However, this was never very successful and led in the first place to a comment in 1974 by John Harding in Nottingham:

'There is now a strong body of informed opinion within the experimental community service projects in favour of some change. Courts, it is recommended, should have the power to make two types of community service order. The first as it now stands without a supervision order. The second a new amendment, a community service supervision order in which a person is given a period of statutory supervision alongside the community service order'. (2)

This was not adopted at the time in England and Wales but did become the basis of community service orders in Scotland. Only with the advent of combination orders in the Criminal Justice Act 1991 did the 'mix' of help and supervision, together with community service work, become available as a single sentence.

In spite of the hectic timetable, the problems of understanding, the varied introductions and suspicion from several quarters, it soon became apparent that community service would maintain its appeal in most criminal courts. Additionally it was shown to be viable in the sense that the majority of offenders made subject to an order completed the hours of work which had been given. Magistrates around the country began to ask that it should be available in their courts and probation services were soon under pressure to ensure that the scheme was available nationwide.

The Home Office research under Ken Pease supported the view that 'The community service experience shows that the scheme is viable'. Nearly 1200 orders had been made in the first 18 months and although the researchers expressed some reservations about the longer term effects upon the workers (which so far could not be known) and there was not then any noticeable effect on the prison population, there was enough enthusiasm for the scheme to go national. This was announced in April 1975.

Early experience
It was made possible for schemes to be introduced in Petty Sessions Areas as they were approved by the Secretary of State. Probation Committees were allowed to spend the necessary money, but permission for this was to be allocated by the Inspectorate; a job for which, with limited experience, it was ill-equipped at that time. This was made worse by the fact, previously noted, that the first organisers had not all been noted for their administrative abilities.

Their dedication, flair and willingness to cover deficiencies with enthusiasm and extreme hard work could not be repeated but it was on their experience that the inspectors relied in allocating funds and vetting schemes for approval. The road to general provision in every petty sessions area proved very bumpy and at the end a close examination revealed an undesirable variety in quality. In one respect differences could be clearly identified; there was universal agreement that the Home Office had seriously under-estimated the cost but some county wide schemes were based on the allocated budget, others started more gradually and used the allocated amount to provide a really viable scheme in only some of their petty sessions areas. The under provision in the former areas dogged those schemes for many years.

Even in two areas where there was a gradual introduction, the schemes had to be suspended on the grounds that 'provision could not be made' (for work). The chief probation officers in those areas found themselves at odds with the Minister of State but it did illustrate that better provision must be made and subsequently extra resources were forthcoming. This was not surprising in view of the fact that the Minister had approved the schemes as they had been set up, so logically if they grew there needed to be a proportionate increase in finance to keep them viable on this basis.

The probation service had not been chosen to introduce and manage community service because of its abilities and experience in community work but it was not without knowledge in this field. An increasing number of probation officers had been trained in universities where there were opportunities to share part of the learning experience with students on community work courses of various kinds. In some cases this led to subsequent movement between the two services and even when no such move was made, further training in the other discipline had been possible. Alongside this there were some joint ventures between borstals, the probation service and voluntary organisations that allowed the inmates some parole to undertake 'voluntary' work of various kinds. In Wiltshire an enterprising probation officer had arranged his own experiment with five youths for whom he obtained a six month deferment of sentence on the understanding that they would undertake some specified work for elderly people in need. The experiment was only partially successful because of the limited skills both of these young people and those supervising, but much was learnt about the need for adequate funding of a community service scheme. Experiences of this kind were now studied by the new organisers being appointed to develop units all over England and Wales.

Another influence at work at this time played an important part in the thinking of some organisers and other community service staff. This came from the development of the therapeutic community at the Henderson hospital under Dr Maxwell Jones and the subsequent emergence of 'New Careers' (3). This was largely sponsored in this country by the National Association for Care and Resettlement of Offenders and based on a premise that young offenders could work together to learn skills in dealing with the issues which led to their delinquency. In the process there would be an element of training in how to help others by understanding better their own law breaking experience; a process which put value upon offenders as people with personalities and skills which could be used for the benefit of others.

Inevitably the development of a new service which, on the one hand, was governed by statute and a growing body of case law, and by more than fifty separate probation authorities on the other, meant there were problems to be tackled. To undertake this the Association of Chief Officers of Probation set up a Community Service Committee which was to become the main forum for discussing issues and offering advice. The first task identified was to produce a handbook to give guidance on practical issues and incorporate the rulings and advice as they emerged from the Court of Appeal. In practice this proved very difficult when everyone involved was learning and new problems and answers to them were emerging in very rapid succession. However, the handbook was produced in 1983 and a paragraph in the introduction sums up its purpose:

'The Guide simply aims to be a statement of the best that current experience makes possible in community service practice. It is intended for the use of practitioners and those concerned in operating and developing schemes for community service by offenders, and is intended to be a working document. While attempting to work towards nationally accepted standards and common practice wherever possible the compilers have also attempted to recognise the need for flexibility where options exist between different principles and philosophies. The Guide is commended by the Association of Chief Officers of Probation for use within all probation areas but its only authority is such as is merited by the quality of its contents.' (4)

The guide at this stage was able to incorporate the results of the initial monitoring of the pilot areas and to take account of detailed Home Office advice in circulars and in particular the memorandum of guidance issued in October 1974 which gave impetus to the detailed planning in all probation areas. One point in this memorandum was to change dramatically with the publication of National Standards in 1989; it concerned breaching defaulting offenders. Paragraph 45 of the memorandum stated:

'The breach procedure provides a sanction against defaulting offenders but it seems likely that community service organisers will seek to bring formal proceedings only as a last resort and will aim, so far as is in their power, to avert situations in which the need to take proceedings might occur.' (5)

Clearly the intention in 1974 was that emphasis should be placed on getting the work done in the hours allocated but in the discussions leading to the issuing of National Standards it was repeatedly stressed that community service was a punishment and that discipline must be imposed to ensure that it felt like a punishment. At the end of discussions with representatives of the Central Council of Probation Committees, ACOP and NAPO, the emphasis on punishment was again greatly modified and made subject to the statement of objectives which starts 'The main purpose of a community service order is to re-integrate the offender into the community'. However, the steps to breach action are spelt out in such a way that the discretion implicit in the 1974 memorandum is greatly reduced.

Community service and juvenile offenders
The Home Office memorandum had made no mention of age in relation to suitability for a community service order or in allocation of types of work. However, many community service committees were anxious that immature young men might be difficult to control and need considerable supervision. As a result some organisers found or developed work specifically for seventeen or eighteen year olds which would recognise their lower level of skill, give them closer supervision to cope with their likely more volatile behaviour, and keep them from the bad influence of older and more experienced criminals. In practice this soon proved difficult to organise and sustain and so seventeen year olds were absorbed into the selection procedures which applied to all. The possibility of contamination from more knowledgeable criminals was more than balanced by the good experience of working alongside more experienced workers with greater

skills.

When, with the Criminal Justice Act 1982, the age was reduced to sixteen, it was quite readily accepted on the basis that it was quite difficult to differentiate between sixteen and seventeen year olds. At that time there was a difference in the maximum number of hours; for 16 year olds it was 120 hours against an 'adult' maximum of 240 hours. However, even this was to change in the Criminal Justice Act 1991 when 240 hours became the maximum for all. In practice this caused little concern in most probation areas, since, in any case the usual number of hours ordered is well below the maximum.

The Wootton Committee seems to have assumed that community service would be a penalty for 'adults' or at least those dealt with in the adult courts, but since 1969 there has been semi-formal provision for community service by juveniles in schemes of intermediate treatment and informal disposals through the development of arrangements for diversion from the criminal justice system. The development of these ideas has been patchy and they have tended to depend upon the enthusiasm of individual probation officers or social workers, but with fresh impetus for cautioning when a Home Office Circular was issued in July 1991 more interest has emerged for diversion schemes in which children make some reparation to victims or undertake tasks which make some repayment to society. This differs from community service in that there are no sanctions if the work is not done. An agreement to undertake some work cannot of course be a condition of a caution but the fact that an arrangement exists does give police officers more encouragement to exercise their option to caution.

Work of this sort cannot be too demanding or require great skill unless the supervising agency is willing to invest in skilled supervisors but that can mean that the bulk of the work is done by the supervisor and the intention of the arrangement is thwarted. The kind of development which has brought a measure of success has occurred when a young shoplifter has apologised to the shopkeeper and undertaken to stack shelves as reparation. Even in this sort of case it is likely that the meeting face to face and the apology are what is most important; it is certainly a chastening experience in most instances.

Community service and fine default

The Wootton Committee did not put forward any very firm proposal for community service for fine default and was satisfied with the one sentence in paragraph 37, 'It might also be appropriate as an alternative to imprisonment in certain cases of fine default.'

Over several years the debate has continued in relation to the use of community service as an alternative to imprisonment for fine default. The possibility of this was introduced in section 49 Criminal Justice Act 1972 but has never been activated in spite of a number of suggestions that it should be, notably by the Parliamentary All Party Penal Affairs Groups in 1980. There has been wide agreement that the wording of section 49 makes the proposal quite unworkable but no amendment has ever been introduced.

The difficulties have been pointed out on a number of occasions (notably by West 1978, Pease 1981 and a report by the Central Council of Probation Committees in 1980). They include problems surrounding the ability to 'buy time' by paying off the fine—or part of it; the increased administrative problems

27

of accounting for the money; the issues of discipline and breach action with lack of sanctions if the offender always has the ability to buy out; the difficulty of inculcating commitment in what would usually be a very short period; problems in relation to placements with other organisations when they would be of short and sometimes unknown duration. Taken all together this list makes it clear that the community service scheme as a whole could be brought into disrepute as a result of confusion in administration caused by differing people being expected to collect the fines whenever payment was offered. However, West (now Roberts) additionally pointed out that the procedures involved in fine default make it apparent there is virtually no point at which it is absolutely clear that a defaulter can be identified, short of the prison gate. Since it is necessary to have the consent of the offender before making the order, and there would need to be an assessment of his/her suitability it is not surprising that the Central Council concluded:

'We are aware that provision for the use of community service in relation to fine defaulters was included in the Criminal Justice Act 1972. This became legislation on the basis of faith as at that time experience was not available upon which to test out the soundness of the concept. The position has now changed completely and as a result of involvement in all the complexities of launching and running community service schemes throughout the country, the Members of the Council feel able to express views on a pragmatic basis that was not possible in 1972.'

The Council went on to reject the concept of community service for fine default.

Summary
Community service by offenders was carefully argued and tested before it came to be put into practice but thereafter change has been rapid and almost continuous. First, there was expansion nationwide, then its introduction for juveniles, and then the statutory requirements of National Standards. In parallel, thinking about the kinds of work offered, the balance between individual placements and work undertaken in groups, and the ways in which the whole experience could best be used to prevent reoffending have all ensured that nothing stays still. Any chapter on the history of change, as this is, must also acknowledge that such change is far from complete.

REFERENCES

(1) *Non-Custodial and Semi-Custodial penalties.* Advisory Council on the Penal System report. HMSO, London (1970)

(2) *Community Service by offenders—the Nottinghamshire experiment,* Harding (ed). NACRO, London (1974)

(3) For an account of this development see 'In place of prison' by Dennie Briggs (1975)

(4) *Community Service Practice Guide.* Association of Chief Officers of Probation, Wakefield (1983).

(5) Home Office Circular 197 of 1974

Chapter 3 Assessing the Impact of Community Service—Lost Opportunities and the Politics of Punishment

Mark Oldfield

Any attempt to assess the impact of community service over the last 20 years is both messy and imprecise since the ambiguous nature of community service leaves its use and value open to a variety of readings. It is, from a probation service perspective, a widely perceived success (Varah, 1987, p 68), offering a means by which offenders may make reparation to the community whilst undergoing a rehabilitative experience within a framework of punishment. This is obviously a penal measure with something for everyone, with the intended effect upon the offender shaped by one's particular position in the criminal justice system.

Despite its apparent success, however, it may be just a little too self congratulatory for the probation service to look back on 20 years of community service as signalling two decades of a more enlightened penal policy. Indeed, it may be argued that (a) community service has made little overall impact on the use of imprisonment by courts, (b) that the use of community service has provided magistrates and judges with a sentence which accords more with an ideological stance toward punishment, thus enabling them to use community service where they would otherwise have used a *less* punitive sentence, and (c) that the popularity of community service amongst sentencers has enabled a smoother transition toward the 'Justice' model within the criminal justice system with the emphasis in future likely to be on creating more punitively interventive disposals, a move signalled by the Criminal Justice Act 1991. In arguing this, I want to locate the use of community service within an overall social policy context of increased bureaucratic control and discipline—both of offenders and staff.

Community service was intended as an alternative to custody but prompts the question of what exactly an alternative to custody would be? Such an alternative sentence would normally be a disposal which is made when the sentencer has originally decided upon passing a custodial sentence upon an individual. It requires an evaluation of the gravity of the case and a decision which allows someone facing custody to receive a disposal in the community. The key question here is who makes that decision? Obviously it is the sentencer. But who has been given the job of providing these alternatives? Step forward the probation service. This disjuncture between policy objectives and the decision making process has marked the failure of government over a long period to actually create genuine alternatives to sending people to prison. There is no sign that government's reluctance to intervene in the sentencing process will change: indeed, the government has only recently bowed to pressure from sentencers in adjusting parts of the Criminal Justice Act 1991.

Community service has, then, been portrayed as providing punishment with elements of reparation and retribution. As an alternative to custody it appeals to those in the criminal justice system aware of the damaging effects of imprisonment and the failure of custodial sentences to prevent further reoffending. It appeals further to those in the criminal justice system who are perhaps not quite as consistently worried by these effects but who still countenance some more creative disposal that would mark an improvement upon the damaging effects of prison so long as that disposal were seen to be tough and demanding. Importantly, community service offers a cheaper alternative to prison in a climate where the reduction of social variables to market components has become an obsession for central government. Politicians can see the benefits of a disposal that costs twenty-four times less per month than the cost of prison (Home Office, 1992, pp 18 to 20) and can be shown (over the short term) to be at least as effective in terms of further reoffending. However, the internal politics of community service, it has been argued, in seeking to attract increased resources for the probation service, make the achievement of success—in terms of reducing reoffending and subsequent reconvictions—so desirable as to compromise the procedures by which offenders are breached, thus obscuring the real reoffending rate (Vass and Menzies, 1989, p 260).

Community service, then, offers a variety of sentencing aims in one package. The attraction of a punishment based on imposing labour discipline has a highly symbolic value that should not be overlooked when examining the popularity of community service as a penal measure. Other eras have also used, in one form or another, work as a means of introducing discipline into lives thought to be morally impoverished by the absence of regular work. The close proximity in an emergent industrial society of forms of punishment and the organisation of work has been documented elsewhere (Foucault, 1977; Melossi & Pavarine, 1981). Official perceptions of the link between work and social discipline are clear and the inversion of the work ethic into forms of punishment, no matter how that punishment is ideologically glossed, comes to be seen as a necessary corrective for the assumed sloth of unemployed people (Parker, 1989, p 72). Offenders at the inception of the community service scheme were quick to note the rapidity with which work could be found for them once sentenced, compared with the apathetic approach of the authorities toward the provision of paid work (NAPO, 1977, pp 9 to 10).

Work, social order and social control have such a seamless fit in the everyday run of modern society that the increasing pre-occupation in the Criminal Justice Act 1991 with additional means of control is perhaps only surprising in that it has taken so long to arrive. We can surely expect more measures that seek to 'mix and match' non-custodial sentences in ways that offer more control at lower costs, especially to any government whose policies are driven by fiscal expedients. The examples of more punitive non-custodial measures in the United States are hardly inspiring. The concept of 'Smart Sentencing' (the penal version of the neutron bomb which 'leaves the offender intact but destroys the offending behaviour') have been shown to have less impact upon offending behaviour where the emphasis is on control and surveillance rather than on the social work content of such sentences (Clear and Byrne, 1992). A case of more not always meaning better. The symbolic utility of work as a penal sanction is also called into question in an age when the amount of waged work is fast declining and its meaning for economically and socially marginalised sections of the population is different from that of the more advantaged in regular work (Jordan and Jones, 1988). Whilst community service may well be seen by those who administer it as an introduction or reintroduction into the work ethnic (Nicholson, 1985), this will increasingly serve little purpose in areas where the chances of finding work are remote. How meaningful then does work performed for 'the community' become, when the very notion of community is reduced to a nostalgic device rather than a meaningful concept? (Rojek, Peacock and Collins, 1987, p 158). We may well see over time a process where community based sanctions become stripped of therapeutic/social work components to be replaced by elements aimed at control and discipline, a process which, too, seems marked by the introduction of the Criminal Justice Act 1991. After all, why inculcate work habits for those who may never get a job?

Community service was, from the beginning, a disposal with a cluster of meanings which offered something to almost everyone with its elements of punishment, retribution and rehabilitation (Young, 1979) and *Table 1* shows how orders made have more than doubled in the last 12 years, even after the first, sustained period of growth might have been expected to subside.

This openness of community service to a multiplicity of readings allowed sentencers to move in the direction of punishment through work—keeping idle hands busy was always likely to be appealing. For the less punitive, there was the rehabilitative element, with the promise of self improvement through the completion of worthwhile tasks for those whose lives had been marked by an absence of being valued and by a lack of opportunity to contribute positively to their communities. Finally there was reparation, paying back the debt of damage done to society, a visible symbol of retribution which expiated the offender through his or her labour. This last notion obviously found resonance when National Standards were first discussed and it was proposed that all those given community service orders above 60 hours should be liable to perform demanding manual work to improve their neighbourhoods. As with all 'tough' measures, however, there is always a feeling in those who support them that they are not tough enough (Parker, 1989, p 66). It is also debatable whether sentencers should be exhorted to use a particular disposal by making it tougher (Clear and Byrne, 1992, p 327). There are indications that toughness sets offenders up to fail and is therefore a poor policy objective since it merely propels offenders higher and deeper into the criminal justice system.

Whichever of the various reasons attracted the actors in the criminal justice system to community service as a disposal, they were overlaid with the possibility of it serving as an alternative to custody. Indeed, it was this aim which has been the subject of debate ever since. Before examining the reasons why community service has never operated as a coherent and unified alternative to custody, it is worth examining what a genuine alternative would be.

Table 1

Community service orders—Commencements 1979 to 1991

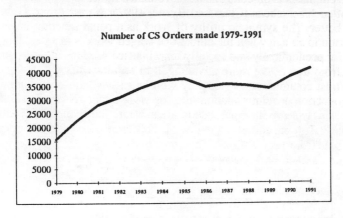

Number of CS Orders made 1979-1991

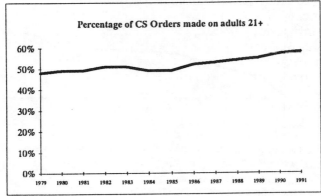

Percentage of CS Orders made on adults 21+

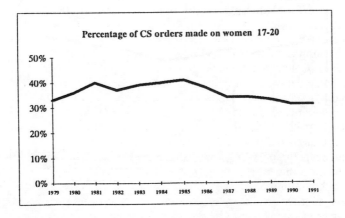

Percentage of CS orders made on women 17-20

Table 1 (continued)

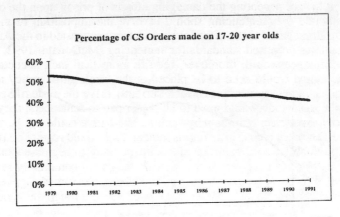

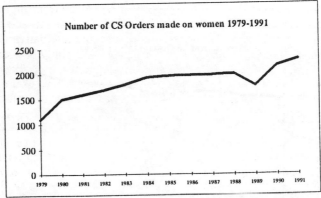

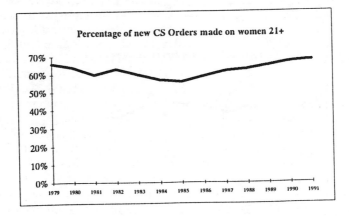

Firstly any real attempt to divert offenders from custody would require some commitment toward accepting the damaging effects of prison upon the offender and the principle that sentencing should involve the imposition of measures which do the 'least harm' to the offender such as those suggested in the American Bar Association's proposed standards for sentencing (McDonald, 1992, p 187). Such an acceptance would, moreover, require more than tacit acceptance by policy makers and would need to be placed at the forefront of policy making, ahead of the economic imperatives which currently drive the system. Secondly, an alternative to custody would need to be prescribed to sentencers: they would need to provide concrete reasons why such an alternative could not be made in cases where they were considering imprisonment. This would require consistency between courts and would need an independent body to regulate sentencing practice, such as a sentencing council. In short, the use of community sentences as alternatives to custody would be a policy objective from the government downwards rather than some vague hope to be achieved through the goodwill of sentencers.

As an alternative to custody, community service was from the outset met with a varied response. The Wootton Committee itself both was and was not in favour of the use of community service as a custodial alternative (Pease and McWilliams, 1980, p 6), feeling that although the order could be used in cases where custody would otherwise have resulted it might also usefully serve as an alternative to other non-custodial measures such as the fine. The Court of Appeal stipulated that not only was community service an alternative to custody but that it was to be seen as a last opportunity to the offender who could have no complaints upon a subsequent appearance in court if a custodial sentence were to be imposed (Young, 1978, pp 128 to 129). The Home Office hoped that community service would be used as a custodial alternative but made no real attempts to achieve this, maintaining sentencers' independence to sentence in as diverse and idiosyncratic way as they chose.

Amongst sentencers, attitudes towards community service have been mixed. One magistrate interviewed demonstrated her own approach to sentencing consistency when interviewed by Vass in saying 'I may regard it [community service] as an alternative to imprisonment but that doesn't mean that I use it in that sense' (quoted in Vass, 1984, p 73). Another magistrate in the same survey thought that at least 60% of offenders on community service were not there as an alternative to custody and that many were diverted from fines. The considered inability to pay a fine rendered the offender susceptible to a community service order since community service could 'provide a useful alternative'.

If official and judicial attitudes toward the tariff position and use of community service were at best ambivalent, offenders being considered for such orders were left in no doubt by probation officers that they were likely to be imprisoned if they did not consent to a community service order: 'At interviews we always tell offenders that the order is an alternative . . . in order to get agreement . . .' (quoted in Vass, 1984, p 79). Certainly probation officers themselves were divided in their attitudes toward community service as an alternative to custody.

Table 2

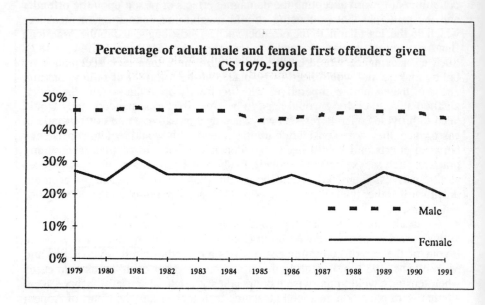

Table 3

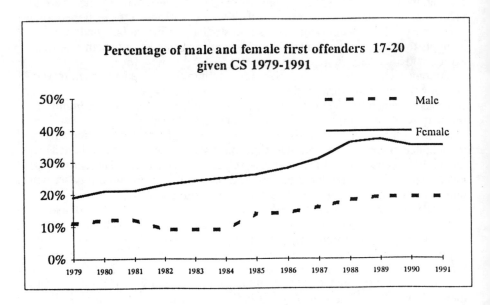

Table 4

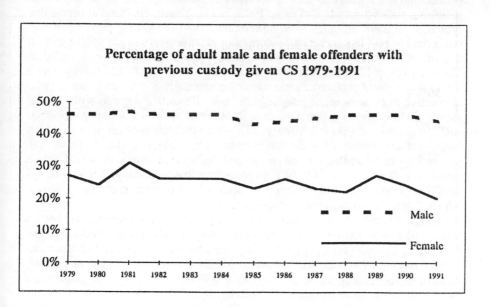

Percentage of adult male and female offenders with previous custody given CS 1979-1991

Table 5

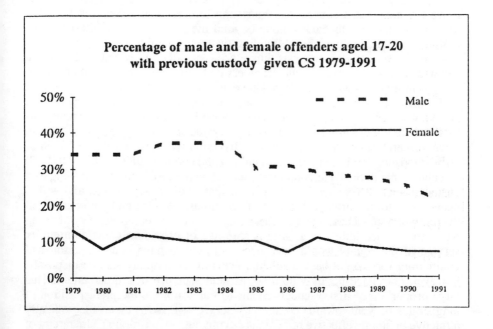

Percentage of male and female offenders aged 17-20 with previous custody given CS 1979-1991

During the early years of the scheme Pease found that over half of probation officers did not regard community service as a sentence in the same way as did their area policy towards it (Pease, 1975, p 33). Young (1978) also found that probation officers' attitudes were mixed and a NAPO working party itself was concerned in case less serious offenders 'should be deprived of the opportunity of a form of disposal which may be particularly suited to their need' (cited in Young, 1978, p 128). More recently Skinns contrasted an ACOP survey which found that 86% of probation areas viewed community service as 'either a strict alternative to custody or, at least, a high tariff disposal' compared with Skinns' survey findings showing that 37% of staff questioned saw community service as such an alternative (Skinns, 1990, p 77). As an indication of the way in which both of these points of view have been met, *Tables 2* and *3* record the proportions of first offenders given community service orders, of which only a small percentage are likely to be a direct alternative to custody; *Tables 4* and *5* look at the opposite end of the spectrum with offenders given community service who had already served a custodial sentence.

This ambiguity about the tariff positioning of community service has been a serious flaw in its use, since the official line was that it could be used instead of immediate imprisonment but it could also be used how and when the sentencer liked. Community service was thus represented as a serious penal sanction, the last stop before prison, but was always available wherever judges or magistrates thought it might be appropriate. Offenders might be given community service for a variety of reasons, often not as an alternative to custody but as a low tariff disposal.

The recognition of community service ostensibly as a high tariff measure, however, meant that subsequent court appearances could well result in the offender being seen as having gone beyond the pale—since an alternative to custody had failed to prevent reoffending there was nothing for it but to impose custody. Community service was thus placed, or rather allowed to settle into a 'net widening' role, moving some offenders up tariff with a subsequent danger of being sent to prison which would not have arisen had they received, say a fine.

Empirically it is difficult to evaluate the impact of community service on custodial sentencing since sentencers have never been required to make returns as to when they have imposed community service in lieu of a prison sentence. Some research suggested high levels of diversion from custody in the region of 70% (Godson, 1981) and, in Scotland, 78% (Duguid,1982). McIvor (1990) calculated that in Scotland community service was subsequently decreasing as a custodial alternative. Clearly, given the disparity of views between and within agencies as to the tariff positioning of community service and the consequent diversity of approaches to its use, there can be no clear cut answer. Certainly, in Kent, experience indicates a large percentage of offenders given community service in the county would have been unlikely to have gone to prison had community service not been available. Previous community service disposals, however, correlated highly with a subsequent sentence of imprisonment. This large proportion of first offenders seems to point more to the predisposition of magistrates in Kent towards community service—it is for them, ideologically attractive or simply effective rather than occupying any position in a hierarchy of sentencing.

Statistical data compiled from probation service returns to the Home Office show that the proportion of young adult offenders aged 17 to 20 who had a previous custodial sentence (and were therefore at greater risk of a custodial sentence if reconvicted) fell between 1979 and 1991 by 13%. The proportion of first offenders (and therefore less liable to a prison sentence) rose during the same period by 8%. For adult offenders the situation was less dramatic, with the percentage of those having a previous custodial sentence falling by 2% and that of first offenders increasing by the same amount. (*Tables 2* to *5* again refer).

Clearly the existence of previous convictions or a lack of them is in itself a crude indicator of offence seriousness. If we look at offence types between 1979 and 1991 as shown in *Tables 6* to *8*, there has been a 3% fall in the number of burglars on community service, a 15% fall in the number convicted of theft and handling stolen goods, a 1% increase in criminal damage and a doubling of the proportion of 'other' and summary offences to 39%. This is hardly an increase in the 'heavy end' offenders who might be thought to be specifically targeted towards community service.

The evidence is, then, that the types of offenders and offence types do not indicate an increase in severity as they might have done had community service been making inroads into the numbers sent to prison. *Tables 9* and *10* compare rates of imprisonment with the proportion of first offenders given community service each year for the period 1981 to 1990. The tables show that, for most of the period the increasing numbers of such offenders accompanied the rising rate of imprisonment. It seems then, that, far from making an impact on the use of custody, community service was actually operating in a 'net-widening' role, taking in offenders who would otherwise have received a less interventive sentence. Certainly at this impressionistic level—bearing in mind that previous convictions alone are a crude way of comparing offenders—community service could hardly be claimed to have acted as an alternative to custody. More properly it was an *accompaniment* to the rising imprisonment rate, allowing sentencers to move the sentencing process up a notch on the punitive ladder. In short, community service has added to the sentencing arsenal without reducing the numbers going to prison.

The use of community service as a disposal for women has been challenged by Dominelli (1984, p 100) for its 'familialist' assumptions about women and the kind of work suitable for them. Certainly the Home Office statistics show that female offenders commencing community service were, from the start, less heavily convicted than men and have become steadily less so. Young women aged 16 who had a previous custodial conviction represented 7% of all such orders in 1985, whilst in 1991 the figure was 2%. Sixteen-year-old female first offenders increased from 20% in 1981 to 34% in 1991. For women aged 17 to 20 there has been a 6% fall in the percentage with a previous custodial sentence from 15% in 1981 to 7% in 1991. First offenders in this age group increased from 21% to 35%. This gives some indication of the differential use of community service from the beginning, with the percentage of young female offenders having a previous custodial sentence around two thirds less than their male counterparts.

Table 6

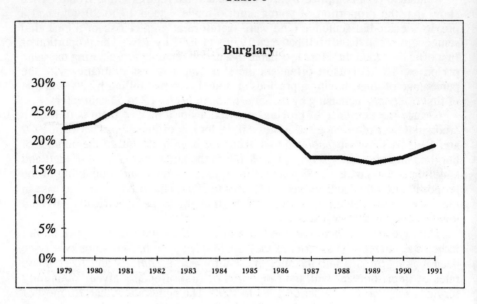

Burglary

Table 7

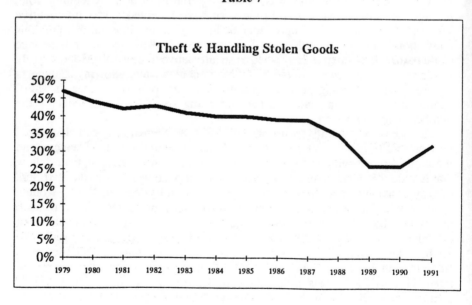

Theft & Handling Stolen Goods

Table 8

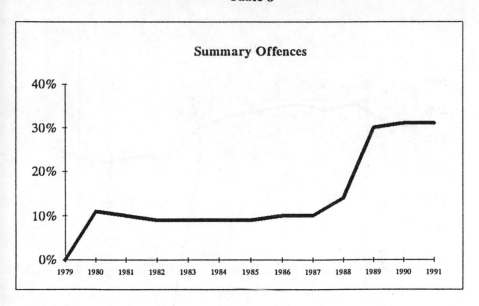

Summary Offences

Table 9

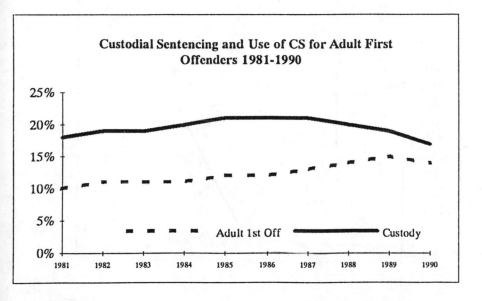

Custodial Sentencing and Use of CS for Adult First Offenders 1981-1990

Table 10

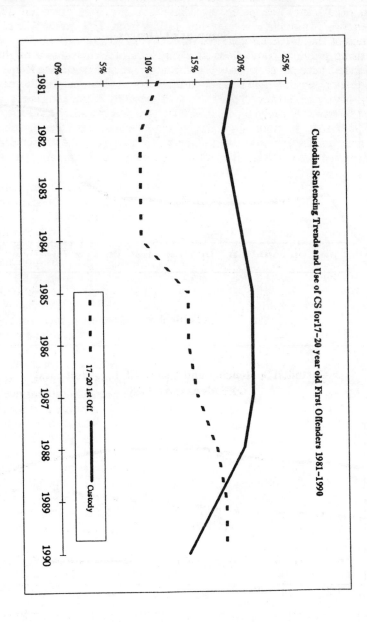

Custodial Sentencing Trends and Use of CS for17–20 year old First Offenders 1981–1990

For women aged over 20 the proportion with previous custody fell from 31% in 1981 to 20% in 1991 whilst first offenders increased from 16% to 28%. For women of all ages the percentage having a previous custodial sentence commencing community service has fallen from 23% to 16% whilst the proportion of first offenders has risen from 18% to 30%.

By using previous convictions as a yardstick of seriousness it might seem that offenders have not necessarily become any more serious despite Home Office and probation service intentions regarding the sentence as an alternative to custody. It may be, however, that the use of previous convictions is too crude a measure by which to gauge the relative seriousness of offenders and assumptions should, therefore, be made with caution. Nonetheless, it is clear that there has been a growing tendency for first offenders to be given community service and it does seem that such offenders would, in the absence of community service as a disposal, have received a lesser sentence.

What of community service once the orders are made? Terminations of community service orders between 1976 and 1991 show a fall of 11% in the proportion of orders completed successfully, with a corresponding increase in orders terminating through reconviction or failure to comply with the terms of the order. Whilst the success rate of community service reached a low point in the year following the introduction of National Standards, no correspondence can be assumed between the two events since the decline was a steady one throughout the period rather than the sudden result of a tightening of administrative procedures. One explanation for the falling success rate could be that the types of offender receiving community service were increasingly more serious and likely to receive a custodial sentence. The increasing proportion of such serious offenders commencing community service with all the attendant problems such offenders often have would, therefore, account for the fall in the success rate. This does not, however, seem to be borne out by the evidence available concerning the type of offender commencing community service during this time. Using the possession of a previous custodial sentence as a measure of seriousness and the likelihood of subsequent custody would indicate a fall in offender seriousness between 1976 and 1991 (Home Office, 1991, pp 93 to 95).

Of course such crude measures are unable to tell us how many cases represent a diversion from custody nor are we able to compare the relative seriousness of cases using measures such as 'risk of custody' scales. The Home Office figures do, though, show that community service is popular, with 8.8% of all disposals in 1991 being community service orders. The number of orders made during 1991 represented the highest use ever, some 47% higher than in 1981 (Home Office, 1992, p 37).

The extent to which community service has been used as an alternative to custody, then, is debatable. It has, however, become a popular disposal—for whatever reason—with sentencers. In 1989, however, the government introduced National Standards for community service, signalling a move toward standardising practice across probation services, and reflecting a concern over diversity in the way community service schemes were being run throughout the country.

The introduction of National Standards set out to spread best practice throughout probation areas. It is useful, however, if National Standards are located within the government's overall social policy strategy since 1979 which Jordan has called 'Authoritarian Benthamism' (Jordan, 1992). Authoritarian Benthamism involves schemes for the regulation and surveillance of problem areas of social life where the 'natural' mechanism of the market or the patriarchal authority of the family fails to hold sway. In such an approach it is considered vital to have centralised regulation using sets of detailed rules and regulations, with their application ensured through detailed monitoring and inspection. Examples of such prescriptive guidelines, argues Jordan, are to be seen in the national curriculum, the social fund manual, the Children Act regulations and of course National Standards for the probation service. The effectiveness of staff operating such systems becomes measured by their ability to conform to the procedures laid down by central authority. This enables the use of a standardised monitoring system which measure conformity and ability to carry out prescribed duties which then are translated into performance indicators. Regulation and surveillance are consequently exercised over both users of the service and staff.

Jordan's model is useful and instructive, since it locates National Standards within a wider approach to the reconstitution of the public sphere along ideological lines. The official rhetoric which underpinned National Standards was that they would enable sentencers to have more confidence in community service as an alternative to custody since they would be assured of its punitive content. (The notion that community based disposals should become ever more punitive is further developed in the Criminal Justice Act 1991). In the Home Office circular introducing National Standards it is made clear that 'the educative or rehabilitative aspects of community service work should not take precedence over the need for the offender to comply with the requirement of a court order'. (Home Office, 1989, para 3). From now on, the positive effects of community service are regarded as a by-product, a spin off from the real purpose of the order which is compliance with its terms. Research such as McIvor's (1991a) which found that the impact of community service upon recidivism was linked to the perceived worth of tasks undertaken counts for little alongside an approach emphasising the application and operation of a set of regulations.

The Home Office circular on National Standards pointed out that 'there seems to be some uncertainty about the standing of community service as a sentence'. (Home Office, 1989, para 4) going on to clarify matters by referring to the Court of Appeal judgments which had indicated the commensurability of community service with a term of imprisonment, though shorter community service orders could be seen as sentences in their own right for offences which would not normally have attracted a custodial sentence. The opportunity to define the use of community service once and for all as a high tariff disposal was not grasped, leaving community service in the 'is it or isn't it?' position it had always occupied. In particular, the contribution community service might make to moving offenders up tariff after further offending was not addressed, despite the Court of Appeal's earlier comments regarding imprisonment after the 'last chance' of community service. The purpose of National Standards spelt out in the circular to probation services, was 'to contribute toward winning the confidence of all criminal courts' (Home Office, 1989, para 37). The tightening of breach procedure would, then, presumably result in a sudden increase in offenders brought back before the courts. How this would contribute toward inspiring confidence amongst sentencers in community service as a disposal is difficult to grasp, since it would have the effect of equating community service with failure. McWilliams points out that in one area where breach procedures were tightened prior to National Standards, the breach rate rose to around four times the national average but this was not accompanied by any rise in the number of community service orders made (McWilliams, 1989, p 123).

The overall emphasis on community service as punishment is evidenced in the way that in the original National Standards the strict regulation of the order becomes more important than the type of work undertaken. The requirement of 21 hours manual work to be included in all orders pays no attention to notions of matching offenders with work in order to produce positive effects. Punishment is stressed to the detriment of all else despite (for example) McIvor's finding that work perceived as worthwhile and positive had the most satisfactory effect on offenders but was still seen by those offenders as punishment, in terms both of imposition of work and deprivation of liberty (McIvor, 1992, p 144).

The second issue of National Standards for community service, which coincided with the Criminal Justice Act 1991, went some way to introducing a more balanced approach. Paragraph 5.9, headed 'Arranging work placements' reads:

'Probation services should arrange a variety of community service work placements for offenders: these should be demanding in the sense of being physically, emotionally or intellectually taxing; of benefit to the community and, if possible, personally fulfilling for offenders and designed to secure public support for the supervision of offenders in the community. Many imaginative and innovative approaches to community service work are possible—and are to be encouraged—consistent with ensuring good quality placements that are sustainable and well managed, that can demonstrate the worth of community service work and that have regard for the perception of community service by those outside the probation service. Possible examples of work placements could include work for elderly people or people with disabilities, environmental projects, improvements to the appearance or amenities of a neighbourhood and crime prevention initiatives'. (Home Office, 1992)

The government's wish to be tough on crime whilst reducing the proportion of offenders going to prison did not extend to attempting to regulate the use of community service by sentencers, thus allowing sentencing discrepancies to continue, as courts carried on exercising their discretion over the use of community service. The mechanistic application of a standardised breach system ran the risk of ignoring the fact that offenders given community service, although ostensibly free of major social problems at the start of the order, might encounter a range of problems during the course of the order with a consequent deterioration in their attendance. McIvor (1991b, p 593) found that around half of a sample of community service workers studied did develop such problems and were able to benefit from varying levels of social work help in order to surmount those problems and complete their orders. This research was conducted in Scotland, where the need for some measure of flexibility and discretion in the exercise of breach proceedings had been recognised in the Scottish National Standards. This is not quite the same as the use of combination orders, however, which are rather an attempt to 'sell' community sentences to courts through the inclusion of technical components whose rigorous enforcement signals the toughness of these measures. The use by magistrates of combination orders, especially for first or less serious offenders, further supports the view that such measures are not used in place of custody for serious offenders but rather merely increase the range of punitive options open to sentencers.

This precedence given to punishment over rehabilitation demonstrates a wish to be *seen* to be tough on crime whilst trying to reduce the prison population as a piece of financial pragmatism. Yet, paradoxically, the government may find that it has contributed to a growth in the numbers going to prison: as Clear and Byrne (1992, p 327) point out, attempts to dramatise sentences by toughening them up can lead to penal measures with multiple and contradictory aims. Such measures may increase offenders' chances of going to prison, not through the commission of new crimes, but through offenders' inability to comply with the cluster of restrictions and constraints involved.

The move from 'soft' approaches to working with offenders (Clear and Byrne 1992, p 325) (that is to say approaches relying on the empathetic and person-oriented skills of workers and which require, to a great extent, the co-operation of the offender) to 'hard' approaches which rely upon the vigorous enforcement of technical elements aimed at surveillance and control is one which reduces the offender to a node in a network of enforcement and regulation. This approach raises the possibility of deskilling probation staff, since their job becomes merely the enforcement of procedures and the recording of infractions of rules. It follows that increases in more punitive penal measures geared at punishment in the community will have serious implications for the probation service. This is something that we should keep in mind, particularly since the introduction of the Criminal Justice Act 1991. The large increase in the numbers of community service orders since the commencement of the Act gives cause for concern, particularly since it seems to indicate reluctance on the part of sentencers to make probation orders unaccompanied by extra conditions. In other words, sentencers seem to be more reluctant to make 'welfare' oriented disposals rather than overtly punitive ones. The shortfall in standard probation orders is being made up by combination orders, often on first time and less serious offenders. The increase in the use of community service and combination orders shows the willingness of courts to move toward tougher sentences if they are made available. There is little indication that sentencers have reduced the proportion of offenders going to prison and, in some areas, there are signs that more young offenders have been imprisoned.

Community service has, then, developed as a multi-faceted penal measure and has remained an ambiguous disposal, an alternative and yet not an alternative to custody. It has functioned, rather, as an *accompaniment* to custody. The Home Office, sentencers and the probation service have been confused as to the extent to which community service might be considered a custodial alternative. The punitive and symbolic nature of the disposal is attractive to sentencers, particularly when dealing with working class unemployed young men who, in times of recession, are conceived as having criminogenic potential (Box, 1987, p 137). Community service has become part of a development of bureaucratic and rule bound social policies which aim at control through punitive rule-enforcement. As community service has been toughened up there has been a need to then toughen it up further: meeting perceived wishes by making more restrictive and punitive sanctions whets the appetite for more—as demonstrated by the increasing use of community service and combination orders by magistrates courts. By combining community service with restrictive measures, there is every chance that the positive experience which has been shown to be of benefit to offenders will be lost as probation services attempt to cope with their burgeoning community service caseloads. The danger is that sheer numbers may lead to setting up schemes which expose offenders to meaningless but punitive tasks. The increasing proportion of first offenders being sentenced to community service brings with it the danger that people who would previously have received a lesser sentence may find themselves being sent to prison for failing to abide by the regulations.

It may seem that a gloomy overview has been presented in this chapter. This should not to detract from the positive experience that community service can provide nor decry the effort of community service staff in the probation service. Both have been substantial and impressive. What this chapter has attempted to focus on has been the failure, over 20 years, to grasp the problem of prison overcrowding and to make a truly innovative step toward reducing the number of people sent to prison each year. The government has allowed sentencers to use community service in a haphazard way, particularly for those people whose circumstances have rendered them unable to pay a fine. It reinforces the lack of a rational penal policy. Whilst we continue to lack such a policy we shall continue to have overcrowded prisons, to which we are offered privatisation as a solution. Sentencing practice will not change if sentencers are left alone to get on with it. As Sabol (1990) points out, exhortation is not enough to move sentencers toward policy goals: they will take any new measures and use them toward achieving *their* goals, not those of government or the Home Office.

Rather than toughening up community penalties, government should get tough with sentencers, restricting their discretion in sentencing. This will be unwelcome since the attitude of the judiciary is that sentencing is an individual 'art' (Shaw, 1986, p 7). The danger of allowing sentencing to take place with no rational penal policy to control and shape sentencing policy allows the probation service to be set up as a scapegoat, held responsible for events beyond their control. At a time when social policies are concerned with defining and regulating the operational performance of all public services, it is somewhat strange that the courts should be left untouched by this process. Finally, the shift toward sentences which emphasise surveillance, control and punishment at the expense of addressing recidivism is a further sign of a myopic penal policy in this county. Our obsession with punishment has always been present these last 20 years, alternatives to custody or not. Twenty years of community service or 20 years of lost opportunities? The impact of community service must be judged not only by what has happened but in the light of what might have been.

REFERENCES

Byrne, J M, Pattavina, A (1982) *The Effectiveness Issue: Assessing What Works in the Adult Community Corrections System*, in Byrne et al (eds)(1992)

Byrne, J M, Lurigion, A J, Petersillia, J, (eds)(1992) *Smart Sentencing, the emergence of intermediate sanctions*, London, Sage.

Clear, T R, Byrne, J M, (1992) *The Future of Intermediate Sanctions: Questions to consider*, in Byrne et al (eds)

Cornell, D, Rosenfield, M and Gray Carlson, E (eds)(1992) *Deconstruction and the Possibility of Justice*, London, Routledge

Dominelli, L (1984) *Differential Justice, Domestic Labour, Community Service and Female Offenders*, Probation Journal, vol 31, no 3, p101-103

Duguid, G (1982) *Community Service in Scotland: the First Two Years*, Edinburgh, Scottish Office Central Research Unit

Foucault, M (1977) *Discipline and Punish: The Birth of the Prison*, London, Penguin

Gates, H L, (1992) *Statistical Stigmata*, in Cornel et al

Godson, D, (1981) *Community Service as a Tariff Measure*, Probation Journal, vol 28, no 4, p124 to 129

Harding, J (1987) *Probation and the Community*, London, Tavistock

Home Office (1989) Circular 18 of 1989 'National Standards for Community Service Orders', London, HMSO

Jordan, W (1992), *Authoritarian Benthamism, Probation in its Social Policy Context*, in Williams, B and Senior, P (eds)

Jordan, W and Jones, M (1988) *Poverty, the Underclass and Probation Practice*, Probation Journal, vol 35, no 4, p123 to 127

McIvor, G (1992) *Quality Counts*, Probation Journal, vol 39, no 3

McIvor, G (1990) *Community Service Orders: Assessing the Benefit to the Community*, Social Work Research Centre, University of Stirling

McIvor, G (1990) *Community Service and Custody in Scotland*, Howard

48

Journal, vol 29, no 2, May 1990, p101 to 113

McIvor, G (1991a) *Social Work Intervention in Community Service*, British Journal of Social Work, vol 21, no 6, p590 to 609

McIvor, G (1991b) *Community Service Work Placements*, Howard Journal, vol 30

McWilliams, W (1989) *Community Service National Standards: Practice and Sentencing*, Probation Journal, vol 36, no 33, p121 to 126

Melossi, D, Pavarine, M (1981) *The Prison and the Factory*, Basingstoke, MacMillan

NAPO (1977) *Community Service Orders, Practice and Philosophy, the report of a working group of the professional committee of NAPO*, Surrey, National Association of Probation Officers

Nicholson, D (1985) CS: *Turning Burglars into Businessmen?*, Probation Journal, vol 32, no 33, p100 to 102

Parker, H, Sumner, M, Jarvis, G (1989) *Unmasking the Magistrates, the 'custody or not' decision in sentencing young offenders*, Milton Keynes, Open University Press

Pease, K, McWilliams, W, (1980) *Community Service by Order*, Edinburgh, Scottish Academic Press

Rojek, C, Peacock, G, Collins, S (1987) *Received Ideas in Social Work*, London, Routledge

Sabol, W J, (1990) *Imprisonment, Fines and Diverting Offenders from Custody: Implications of Sentencing Discretion for Penal Policy*, Howard Journal, vol 29, no 1, p25 to 41

Shaw, R (1986) *The Probation Service in a Flawed Justice System*, Probation Journal, vol 36, no 1, p 5 to 11

Skinns, C D, (1990) *Community Service Practice*, British Journal of Criminology, vol 30, no 1, p 65 to 80

Varah, M, (1987) *Probation and Community Service*, in Harding, J (ed)

Vass, A A, Menzies, K (1989) *The Community Service Order as a Private and Public Enterprise, a comparative account of practices in England and Ontario, Canada*, British Journal of Criminology, vol 29, no 3, p 253 to 272

Vass, A A, (1984) *Community Service Orders: close encounters with a penal substitutue,* St. Ives, Venus Academica

Williams, B, Senior P, (1992) *Probation Practice After the Criminal Justice Act 1991,* PAVIC, Sheffield City Polytechnic

Young, W, (1970) *Community Service Orders: the Development and Use of a New Penal Measure,* London, Heinemann

Chapter 4 Working It Off

David Scott

'If it wasn't for community service, I wouldn't get out at all'. Just a routine comment by one person about an individual scheme but a recurrent theme of many beneficiaries interviewed about the value of community service. Elsewhere in this book there are important contributions about the effect community service has on the criminal justice system as a whole. This chapter moves behind the concepts, theories and statistics to consider the impact of community service on the lives of real people.

Statistics may inform us, for example, that x-thousand hours are worked each year by men and women on community service but, as sentencers so often want to know, what actually happens once an order is made? This is a glimpse of the many ways in which those hours are worked day by day across the 55 probation areas of England and Wales.

In Birkenhead, on a sprawling industrial estate beset by problems of unemployment, drug abuse and family breakdown, a group of young men wash cars at a community centre. The car drivers have disabilities so keeping their vehicles clean presents difficulties.

Inside the community centre, away from where the cars are washed, a group of elderly people talk about the value of community service for them. One man worked for a firm for 35 years but has no entitlement to an occupational pension. His physical disability is one handicap, his low income another. Having his car washed is a real pleasure, particularly as it inspires good natured envy amongst his neighbours.

There is another source of satisfaction, too. While his car is being washed he meets with others and the friendly banter is as important to him as the state of his vehicle. As they talk, the sessional supervisor employed by the community service unit oversees the work to make sure that the cars are cleaned to a good standard and those on the scheme persevere with the washing and waxing.

Perhaps not surprisingly, the community service workers prefer the scheme to imprisonment. On the day I met them, each of the workers involved had at some time experienced prison and the bitterness about its damage in terms of family life was never far from the surface. For them, community service has value and the cleaning of cars is worthwhile because they can see the benefit of their efforts in the reactions of those in many ways less fortunate than themselves.

Across the city, within a mile of Liverpool football ground, one house in an end row of terraces is owned by a voluntary social services organisation. The community worker, a friendly and humane man, has an open door to the myriad problems around him in the community—debt, violence, alcohol abuse, child abuse—the catalogue goes on. The house is an important focal point for youngsters and the elderly alike, providing refuge for the unemployed, children out of school and others.

Within this environment community service workers are placed to help out. The community worker cannot be too prescriptive about what they should do. For some it will be running activities, for others it will be repairing the building, painting and decorating, or helping out in different ways.

Here community service provides a welcome pair of hands but it is also a route to reintegration into the community. The fact that a man or woman has offended is not in itself a problem because many of the people coming to the centre will themselves have criminal records. This everyday attitude to offending is illustrated by the youngsters who ask the community service worker, 'How many hours you got left then?'. The good relationship built up between the local community service officer and the community worker ensures that any problems are dealt with quickly and effectively.

In another district on Merseyside, at a nursery school, young children between the ages of three and five years play on a wooden train the size of a small truck. The head teacher eyes the train with real satisfaction. It was made by community service workers at the Probation Service workshop, a commercial unit indistinguishable from any other on the local factory estate.

The idea for the train had come about when the head teacher met with a crime prevention police officer, who mentioned that the community service unit might be able to help. In an area where local residents despair of graffiti the train has been undamaged, a factor the head teacher puts down to it being built by men and women on community service who have local connections. Plans are now in hand for more outdoor toys to be built. The head teacher explains that with her equipment budget of £2000 it would have been impossible to buy the train commercially.

Workshops are an important innovation for many services. They enable services to plan the throughput of work more effectively. One of the many tasks taken on by the Wirral community service unit was the making of a special bed for a young victim of cerebral palsy. The youngster had grown out of the old hospital bed he was using and a medical social worker had suggested that the community service unit might help. The hand-built bed features carved panels and two footballers painted on the side.

The perspectives of the mother and the community service manager offer a real insight into the value of community service. The boy's mother described the bed to a local reporter as being 'fit for a king'. She went on to agree wholeheartedly with the value of the unit. 'Something like this is so worthwhile, it helps everyone', she said. Her enthusiasm was matched by the community service manager, an experienced senior probation officer who explained that building the bed had given great pleasure to those working on the project, especially as they were able to deliver it in person.

Another CS unit in the city has undertaken the extensive restoration of a community centre. This has been a major project which has involved CS workers in stripping out and restoring much of the complex. Floors have been replaced, walls and ceilings repaired and decorated and the kitchen redesigned. The sessional supervisor has had a key role in overseeing the work, maintaining discipline and helping offenders to learn and apply skills which many of them were unaware they could achieve prior to the project.

There is little doubt that the sessional staff used by most CS schemes are 'at the sharp end'. Their job description sounds daunting, as are the expectations. Take a group of offenders, many of whom will have limited ability and social skills, most of whom will resent being required to attend and are likely to be suspicious of and resistant to authority—and ensure they produce a good standard of work unpaid and in the public eye.

Inevitably, as with effective relationships between students and teachers, offenders will respond to supervisors with the right 'approach'. The type of work is important but the attitude of the supervisor is critical, the best being firm but fair with an ability and openness to work alongside the offenders whilst retaining sufficient detachment to set standards.

Although the organisation of CS schemes varies, not least between urban and rural areas, a recurrent theme is the need to balance the throughput of offenders made the subject of orders, the work available and the quality of the overall operation. The linkage between supervisors, organisers and managers is vital. If standards slip the confidence of courts, beneficiaries and offenders alike will be lost.

For senior managers and committees there are key strategic decisions to be taken about the resourcing of CS relative to all the other demands falling on a service with a cash limited budget. If the demand for CS increases by 25% in a six month period, as happened in Merseyside around the implementation of the Criminal Justice Act 1991, the options are limited but the action taken critical.

•••••

By contrast with predominately industrial Merseyside, running community service schemes in Wiltshire presents logistics of a different type. Much of the county is rural and travel to and from projects is a factor.

To the north of the county Swindon is a rapidly developing and changing town. In a local shopping area, on an early summer day, 16 stroke victims are being served lunch by community service workers. The atmosphere is light and full of good natured comment. There is an obvious affinity between the victims, most of whom are elderly, and the younger community service workers. The workers' day begins at nine o'clock when they collect the patients in their specially adapted minibus and deliver them to the centre. After preparing lunch the workers will take the patients wheelchair shopping before leading bingo and other activity sessions and returning them home at the end of the day. Many of the patients explain that but for the community service workers and their scheme they would not get out at all.

The Wiltshire service is understandably proud of its community service scheme. From its inception the service has invested in the concept of reparation to the community. In disparaging the 'can you dig or can you paint?' approach to work placements it has used its staff imaginatively to look outwards to the community to identify where the resources of the community service unit could be best directed locally.

The approach pioneered in Wiltshire has been to establish gaps in services provided by statutory and voluntary organisations and to meet areas of previously unmet need. For example the service identified the desperate need for respite care experienced by those with responsibility for children with severe emotional, or physical difficulties, or the elderly housebound. Similarly, it discovered that patients in long stay hospitals had little to occupy them at weekends. After careful discussion with representatives of the local community, trade unions and other organisations, the service has set up and run a series of clubs such as the Stroke Club. The clear value of the scheme to the community has enabled the service to develop sponsorship arrangements which have been used, for example, to provide the specially adapted minibuses used to transport groups of people who require wheelchair access.

Clubs are administered and operated on behalf of the Chief Probation Officer to 'provide work for offenders to the benefit of the local community'. They are regarded as an integral part of the work of the service. Management responsibility is held by the senior probation officer, community service; day to day running of the individual schemes, such as the Stroke Club is the responsibility of the unit probation officer, or the community service officer.

By involving its staff within a clear framework of principles which are owned by senior management and the Probation Committee, the Wiltshire service has developed a very distinctive approach to community service. This has resulted in schemes such as the wheelchair shopping or the Saturday Clubs in which offenders assist in very direct ways with youngsters or adults who have severe learning difficulties, or disabilities. The commitment and initiative of staff was illustrated by the recent holiday which was organised for the Stroke Club.

So often there is an affinity between the old and the young which runs counter to the images portrayed by the popular press. The fact that the community service workers are offenders is well known. Many of the stroke victims empathise, recognising their own waywardness as youngsters, or life's unpredictability.

The Wiltshire service provides a balance of schemes which they categorise as caring or practical. The caring schemes provide about 40% of their total community service hours and these have a better attendance rate than their practical counterparts. Within a broad range of placements, some supervision is provided by the sessional worker employed by the service; in others, the so-called single placement, the beneficiary provides the supervision.

A dip into the work placements on offer, at any one time, gives an idea of the formidable range . . . including, for example, MENCAP, Odstock Hospital, local churches, wheelchair shopping, education centres, and the Salvation Army.

• • • • •

Crawley in West Sussex shares some similar characteristics with Birkenhead and Swindon. All are towns developed since the Second World War. On the outskirts of one of the main districts, some distance from the main centre, lies one of the many housing estates. On the corner of one street adjoining an area of parkland which separates it from the main road, there is a small end-of-terrace flat in which a young single mother and six month old twins have recently been re-housed.

Community service became involved before the re-housing when they helped to renovate the previous substandard rented property. The referral came from a health visitor who has good local contacts with the community service organiser. Since being re-housed the community service unit has cleared the garden of rubbish and dangerous debris and restored and rehung an outside gate. Beforehand the flat seemed derelict because of the dilapidated state of the gate and rubbish thrown into the garden. It is now a source of pride for its occupant, who feels more secure and is pleased that the twins will have a safe play area when they are old enough to use the garden.

How did the young mother feel about having offenders in her home? The answer is simple and direct. They were the only ones who were prepared to help when she was in need. She is full of praise for the community service unit, which has responded whenever she has been concerned. Without community service she could not have afforded to have the work done—a commercial quote of £700 being well beyond her 'pocket'. Another interesting observation follows. The community service workers work hard, rarely stopping even for a tea-break, which draws an unfavourable comparison with their commercial counterparts. Later, on leaving the house, there is an opportunity to reflect with the CS unit that it is hard to put a price on many of the benefits of community service, the added value, which those involved with the scheme often take for granted. In this case, the house is surrounded by drug dealing, so the children's safety and security are a recurrent worry. Making the property more secure has brought peace of mind and contributed to the growing confidence of a young parent at a time of need.

On the edge of Crawley close to the airport there is an adventure playground set in parkland and thriving with activity on an early summer's morning. The play leader is a community service enthusiast. In one corner of the playground is what from the outside looks like an old prefabricated garage. Inside it has been transformed into a venue for table tennis. The adventure playground now has teams playing in five leagues. The 'centre' is in constant use. Before community service became involved this was not the case. In the winter it was unusable due to cold and damp. The community service unit has insulated the walls and ceiling, redecorated the centre and carpeted the floor. Outside in another part of the playground workers have built a quiet area where parents and children can picnic away from the busy activities.

At the entrance to the playground a community service worker on an individual placement has painted a mural on an old caravan to brighten up an area which was becoming an eyesore. The mural depicts worries about threats to the environment and world peace. The same worker is now designing a stage set for an open air theatre. She is surrounded by young children, all of whom have tasks in designing and painting the set.

As she pauses from her work she explains that the value of community service for her is in the work being done. She can see the benefits for the children and is pleased that they have taken to painting with such enthusiasm. Her case has not been straightforward. Involvement with drugs has been a recurrent problem but she is now within sight of completing her order satisfactorily.

Following the intervention of an enthusiastic and creative leader, who was concerned about an increase of criminal damage in the town, the playground almost encourages graffiti. Some of the walls are painted over and over again with new designs, the difference being that instead of this being what the popular press might describe as mindless vandalism, in the context of the playground it is a constructive activity. Further across the town there is another adventure playground, at the entrance to which community service workers are putting the finishing touches to a fort. This is no ordinary project but a major piece of construction which will provide a play setting, a theatre and a location for a variety of activities.

The story behind its construction is interesting. It was designed and largely built by two men who had already completed their community service hours. They bring their children to the centre and are pleased to see the product of their initiative near completion. There is nothing special to them about what they have done. They describe it in a very matter-of-fact way, which provides another illustration of the problem of quantifying the elusive 'added value' of community service. Quite clearly, here too community service has been an important catalyst in providing an amenity which will be of enduring benefit to local youngsters, but where will this ever show in the 'law and order' balance sheet?

On the outskirts of Crawley a derelict farm building provides an unlikely setting for another community service project, which is run in partnership with a local voluntary organisation. At regular intervals throughout the weekend two vans travel to and from an old barn which has become a repository for second-hand furniture. The voluntary organisation provides a service to the local community by collecting unwanted furniture and delivering it on request in the locality. It handles the organisation of the project with the direct labour coming from the community service workers under the direction of the local unit.

All involved see the mutual benefits of partnership. For the voluntary organisation the picture is straightforward; without the input from the community service unit the project could not run.

Community service workers find the project varied and interesting. The work can be exhausting as anyone with experience of handling cumbersome furniture up and down stairs will appreciate. Their perspectives are interesting; frequently, as they observe, they will be taking furniture from houses in sad circumstances of bereavement and delivering to occupants living in conditions of abject poverty. On this Saturday one of the vans is crewed by a woman community service worker. Her experience of the project is very favourable. Initially, she was angered by being given 'woman's work' at an old persons' home. She raised her concerns with the community service officer, who redeployed her to this project.

The CS unit has plans to develop a workshop which will enable it to use workers' hours to restore the furniture before delivering it to those in need. Similar projects operate across the country enabling CS to provide a valuable service at relatively low cost.

• • • • •

In Sheffield the community service unit runs a regular luncheon club for senior citizens, in partnership with the Social Services Department which is the main referring agency. The scheme operates at nine centres across the city on Monday to Friday throughout the year.

At any one time, between 500 and 550 elderly people are 'members' of the luncheon club. Last year, the unit estimates it provided 21,500 meals at a nominal cost of 80 pence each.

Where required to do so, the unit provides transport to and from the clubs. It takes pride in the service it organises. Fresh meals, not prepacked or frozen are supplied daily and although the food is a focal point, the unit sees the value of the club in encouraging a social network for the elderly. At one of the luncheon clubs there is a 'meals on wheels' service in addition to the meals served on the premises.

The community service workers assist in many different ways, transporting club members, preparing the food and assisting with the social activities which are as important as the lunch. Any venture of this type involves risk. When the luncheon clubs began eleven years ago one of the staff's main worries was the potential harm which could befall the elderly, for example theft of belongings. But in eleven years they have simply had no reported incident of theft. The key, as so often, seems to lie in the relationships which are established under the watchful eye of the supervisors. By attending on a regular day of the week, the offenders and senior citizens get to know and have confidence in each other. One 74 year old put it this way: 'We have a lovely time when we come here and the young people are so helpful, it's hard to think that they have been in trouble . . . it's true that old people are frightened to go out at night but coming here does help keep our spirits up. We have found the people here are very kind to us and coming here is the highlight of the week'.

For many disabled people, the highlight of the week is a trip out organised through the Riding for the Disabled scheme. In Kent, the Darenth Park stables were refurbished almost entirely by community service workers, making viable a scheme that would otherwise almost certainly not be available. The same stories could be repeated across all 55 probation areas and an audit of the work accomplished during a typical weekend throughout the country would reveal the astonishing range of projects now being undertaken—large-scale conversation projects and countryside park improvements; churchyard and footpath clearance, refurbishment of village halls and restoration of industrial canals among them. On single placements you could find offenders working unobtrusively but well in charity shops, old people's homes, a nursery school for handicapped children, local re-cycling schemes and sports facilities for young people—coaching them in swimming and athletics.

Many CS schemes make a substantial contribution to the crime prevention work of the service.

• • • • •

In the early seventies when community service began, there was an American detective series which began with an aerial view of skyscrapers and a commentary to the effect 'There are six million stories in this city—this is one of them'. This came to mind in reflecting on this chapter. Each day, across the 55 probation services in England and Wales, community service is being worked in a variety of ways and a range of settings and it is reliant for its undoubted success on the skills of its staff in the way it helps to reintegrate offenders into the community.

In industry, as the commercial world becomes ever more competitive, the search for 'added value' is the holy grail. What practices or processes add value to the operation? The concept of added value is emerging slowly into the public sector and community service provides many examples of its potential usage. How, for example, might the city of Sheffield quantify the added value of 25,000 meals being served annually to elderly citizens in conditions which encourage dignity and fellowship both for the old people and offenders? What price for the youngsters in Crawley enjoying the benefits of the refurbished adventure playground?

Yet so often 'negative equity' is the focus of the criminal justice system. Experts on crime and punishment are never far away.

'But this generation is too wet to return to the wisdom of the ages. There are alternatives, one of which would be to humiliate the young criminals who swagger about housing estates setting such a bad example to smaller children. These young villains should be put to forced labour on rubbish dumps and waste sites. *It is crucial to deglamourise them in the eyes of their peers.*' (*Sunday Express,* 11 July 1993).

The probation service is always vulnerable to the accusation that community service is a soft option, yet it is a beacon for those who believe in a humane criminal justice system. It provides reparation, albeit mostly indirect, to the community which adds value to the well-being of many, often voiceless citizens. However, the one single truth that community service holds above all others is that the process of reintegration into the community is achieved through dignity and self-respect and *not* through humiliation.

Asking offenders to clean up the mess of a materialistic society will alienate and marginalise them further. Demanding them to confront their offending in a way which is challenging but constructive will pay dividends in the longer term.

Chapter 5 Access For Women: Flexible and Friendly?

Jean Hine

' . . . the most successful sentencing innovation since 1945' is how the *Daily Telegraph* describes it, but do female offenders have grounds to feel so positive about community service?

This chapter will examine whether female offenders have the same opportunity to experience community service as male offenders. It will then go on to address whether the implementation of the Criminal Justice Act 1991, which changed the basis of community service as a sentencing option for the courts and specifically includes provisions about equality issues, has improved the access of female offenders to community service.

Numbers of women on community service are small. A look at any community service scheme in the country will demonstrate this. Even though a scheme may have above average proportions of women, they will nonetheless be in the minority. Is this indicative of inequality of access for CS? Uneven numbers do not necessarily demonstrate unfair treatment, in the same way that disproportionate patterns do not equate with discrimination.

In my view, equality of access means that people in a similar situation with respect to offence and previous criminal history have equal opportunity to opt for community service, and should they do so have an equal chance of being sentenced to a similar length community service order. This is over-simplistic and contains a lot of conditions, but it does highlight the fact that a sentence of community service is actually the outcome of a process which has several stages, each of which may impact on equality of access to it. This process and the important stages in it will be the same for all offenders, male and female, but the actual factors influencing that process will be different.

Patterns in sentencing
The latest available national figures (England and Wales) are for the year 1991. They show that, overall, 5% of the females sentenced for indictable offences received a community service order, compared with 9% of the males sentenced. Proportionately then, men are almost twice as likely to be given community service. Raw numbers show an even bigger difference, with 27,587 males receiving an order during that year, compared with 1,906 females. Provisional figures for 1992 suggest an increase to even greater numbers.

Table 1

Table 1 (a) Percentage of male and female offenders sentenced to community service for indictable and summary offences since 1981

Court & Gender		1981	1986	1987	1988	1989	1990	1991
Magistrates'	Female	0.5%	0.5%	0.6%	0.7%	0.5%	0.6%	0.7%
	Male	1.2%	1.7%	2.1%	2.0%	1.9%	2.2%	2.5%
Crown	Female	4.5%	7.1%	6.7%	7.2%	7.5%	9.4%	9.8%
	Male	8.1%	10.2%	10.5%	10.7%	11.1%	13.1%	13.6%
(b) Actual number of females sentenced to community service								
Magistrates'	Female	1278	1438	1378	1384	1112	1397	1506
Crown	Female	272	491	488	551	563	711	404
Total	Female	1550	1929	1866	1935	1675	2108	2210
		17.5	25.5	26.2	28.5	33.6	33.7	31.9

Source: Home Office Statistical Bulletin 13/92 plus personal communication

Table 1 shows how the proportions of male and female offenders sentenced to community service have changed over time. The figures here are based on indictable and summary offences, and thus do not tie up exactly with those mentioned above.

In both magistrates' courts and the Crown Court in all years a higher percentage of males were given community service than were females. The figures for magistrates' courts show little variation in the percentage of females sentenced to CS: those for males show a gradual increase until the late eighties and then a steadying since 1987. The trend in the Crown Court is very different. The female CS sentencing rate more than doubled between 1981 and 1991, and whilst the rate for males increased significantly too, the disparity between males and females shrank. In 1981 women had less than a 1 in 22 chance of being given a community service order when men had a 1 in 12 chance. In 1991 women had a better than 1 in 11 chance compared to men's 1 in 7.5 chance. We can thus say that in the Crown Court at least, female access to community service, measured as the likelihood of receiving an order, has improved.

The figures in part (b) of *Table 1* show that whilst the proportion of sentences coming from the Crown Court has gradually increased and levelled out at the current rate of about a third, the magistrates' courts still make the majority of community service orders received by women.

Home Office *Statistical Bulletin* 17/93 which gives the 'Summary Probation Statistics for England & Wales 1992' shows how the rate of sentencing for probation, community service and custody varies with age. The *Table 2* gives that information for community service, broken down by gender.

The rate of sentencing to community service has increased over the last four years for each of the four groups, and increased at similar rates. The rates are higher for the 17 to 20 year olds for both males and females, but we can see that the differences between the younger and older age groups are much greater for men than for women. Males are roughly twice as likely to be given a community service order if they are aged 17 to 20, ie females are only about half as likely to get one. These figures suggest that the question we should be addressing is not 'why are female sentencing rates so low', but rather 'why is the sentencing rate for 17 to 20 year old males so high'. The attitudes of English society and sentencers towards young adult males have frequently been commented upon, and it may be that community service conveniently meshes with those.

Additional tables were provided to probation services by the Home Office with their copies of the Criminal Statistics Supplementary Tables for 1991. The tables give sentencing figures for each probation area, presenting all defendants sentenced for indictable offences in the area, broken down by age and gender. They allow us to look at the picture around the country on a similar age and gender basis, at least for the one year: see *Table 3*.

In each of the age groups, males were more likely to be given a community service order than were females of the same age. As with *Table 1*, the proportion of males given community service declines with age, whereas for females the proportions in the different age groups are much the same. There is wide variation between probation areas in the proportion of community service orders which are given by the courts, for both sexes.

Table 2

Table 2 Offenders sentenced for indictable offences: percentages sentenced to community service by age and gender

Age Group	Gender	1989	1990	1991	1992
17 – 20	Females	4.8%	5.5%	6.3%	6.5%
	Males	12.6%	13.4%	14.5%	15.0%
21 and over	Females	3.0%	3.8%	4.2%	5.1%
	Males	5.8%	6.8%	7.8%	9.0%

Source: Home Office Statistical Dept plus personal communication

62

Table 3

Table 3 Offenders sentenced for indicatable offences (all courts) in 1991: percentage of males and females in each age group who received a community service order

Age Group		Females	Males
17 – 20	England & Wales Overall	6%	14%
	Range	1% – 13%	7% – 23%
21 – 25	E & W Overall	5%	10%
	Range	1% – 15%	8% – 16%
26+	E & W Overall	4%	9%
	Range	1% – 10%	3% – 12%
All ages	E & W Overall	5%	9%
	Range	1% – 8%	6% – 15%

Source: Criminal Statistics England & Wales, 1991, Additional tables

A search for correlations in the data could prove interesting, but this has not been possible for this analysis. Simple scanning of the figures shows however that there is no simple pattern: the areas with the highest proportion of community service for males of all ages had only slightly above average rates for females of all ages. Within the age bands there was also variation for these areas. Thus a high use of community service for males is not necessarily accompanied by a high use for females: the picture is much more complex.

Patterns in offending

It is well established that the two most important factors in sentencing are (a) the offence(s) for which the offender is sentenced, and (b) the previous criminal history and sentences of the offender. The different pattern of offending for women, both in type and volume, is well documented.

Women are much less likely to be involved in crime than men. Work on criminal careers shows that

'One in three males born in 1953 had been convicted of a 'standard list' offence before the age of 31 . . . The cumulative conviction rates for females are far lower, with seven per cent of those born in 1953 having received a conviction before the age of 31.'

This is equivalent to 1 in 14 females, so men are almost 5 times more likely to receive a criminal conviction than are women.

The Home Office publication 'Gender and the Criminal Justice System' provides a useful overview of the extent of female involvement with the criminal justice system. In 1990, 17% of 'known offenders' (ie those found guilty or cautioned for indictable offences) were female, ie less than 1 in 5. The pattern of offences for these known offenders was different: see *Table 4*.

The biggest offence category for both groups was theft, although it was a much higher proportion of male offending than female. Within this category there was also a different pattern, with theft from shops accounting for 71% of women's theft, but only 37% of men's. Women's offences of violence and burglary were very low in comparison. It has been suggested that women have become more involved in crime and that their pattern of offending has changed since their 'liberation' in the 1960s. Malcolm Ramsey examined this thesis in 1984 and concluded—

'Attempts to link 'women's liberation' with increases in female delinquency lack any very substantial foundation . . . To date, those improved opportunities which, to varying degrees, women have enjoyed, may have served not so much to increase the extent or to alter the nature of female delinquency as to stimulate groundless fears about the growth of female delinquence . . . this process may even have helped to change the perceptions of women held by those working in the criminal justice system, and to stiffen their responses to female delinquence.'

Table 4

Table 4 Offences of known offenders

Offence	& of females charged with offence	% of males charged with offence
Theft	2.	3.
Violence	5.	6.
Burglary	8.	9.
Other	11.	12.

Source: Race & Gender in the Criminal Justice System, Home Office 1992

65

The higher incidence of theft among females may explain why cautioning rates are higher overall for females (just under 50%) than for males (about 33%) but this is only part of the explanation. When offence groups are examined individually, females are found to have a substantially higher cautioning rate than males for all offence types except drugs. A variety of explanations are possible: the female offences are less serious, females have less previous convictions than males, or maybe some police practice is discriminatory. Most likely there is a combination of these explanations at play, but the net result is that a smaller percentage of female offenders are charged than males, thus reducing even further the number of women who proceed through the criminal justice process.

A smaller proportion of female offending is dealt with by the Crown Court than male offending (16% compared with 24%). Research by the Home Office Research & Planning Unit has found that this is partly because females are less likely to elect to go to Crown Court. This in itself will reduce their chances of receiving a community service order, as shown in *Table 1*.

Different types of offence attract different types of sentence whatever the gender of the offender or the court. The differential rates of sentencing to community service have often been taken as a reflection of this different offending pattern, but this is by no means straightforward, as the Home Office booklet warns:

'Consistency in sentencing does not mean that all offenders convicted of crimes within a particular offence category should automatically receive the same sentence. Sentencing courts may legitimately take into account a large number of other factors . . . such as seriousness of the particular offence . . . the circumstance of the offence and any other aggravating or mitigating factors. We do not know how far men and women differ on these factors.'

More worrying, however, is the range of other possible explanations which have been put forward, most of which have little to do with the features of the offence and much to do with being female.

In the Crown Court, Moxon found that community service was favoured for offenders with several previous convictions and fairly serious offences such as burglary, robbery and violence. Community service orders were particularly used for younger offenders and Moxon suggested that an older offender in similar circumstances may well have received a suspended sentence of imprisonment. Women were less likely to be in these 'favoured' categories, and thus less likely to be given community service, but interestingly, Moxon also says:

'. . . it was often only the sex of the offender which seemed to tip the balance between probation and community service.'

He suggested that this may in part be due to the way in which women offenders are perceived by the court, quoting the 'mad versus bad dichotomy' of Allen, whereby:

'. . . females were much more likely to be seen as victims of their circumstances and in need of support, males as in control of their circumstances and deserving punishment.'

Anne Worrall's analysis of the processing of female offenders led her to the view that the situation was more complex, and suggested that women can be viewed by courts in two quite different ways:

'. . . women are more likely than men to be processed according to an assessment of their personal circumstances, rather than their offence . . . The machinery for processing female offenders is built on the myth that 'real' women cannot commit 'real' crime. Offenders are placed in one of two categories—'the pathetic menopausal shoplifter' type or the 'sophisticated criminal' type: the former dealt with leniently, the latter severely.'

This scenario, if accurate, leaves little place for community service: the options are either probation (help for the pathetic) or custody (punishment for the sophisticated).

Lena Dominelli's interviews with magistrates, probation officers and community service staff revealed that:

'the main factor considered for women was their domestic role, whilst for men it was their wage earning role.'

This emphasis on domestic circumstances has frequently been cited in relation to women's access to community service. Young suggested that women were often perceived as being personally unsuitable for community service because of personal or domestic instability, pregnancy, dependent children etc, and so community service developed as a male oriented sentence regardless of its position in the tariff.

More recently, work has been undertaken which controlled for offence and previous criminal history in an attempt to assess the impact of gender on sentencing. Mair and Brockington examined cases in two magistrates' courts, matching males and females for age, type of offence and previous convictions. They found that there was very little difference between them in their sentencing pattern, including the likelihood of a community service order.

Sentencing work then can say little about the relationship between previous criminal history, offence and gender in terms of receiving a community service order. On the other hand, all of the material available about the people who are given community service orders shows considerable differences between men and women. 'Probation Statistics for England & Wales 1991' contains a few tables which show some differences and changes over time. The women who get community service are generally older than the men, and whilst the proportion of 17 to 20 year olds has become smaller over the last ten years the trend has been the same for both women and men and thus the difference has remained. The proportion of first offenders among the females who get community service is significantly higher than the proportion among males. The proportion of men who were first offenders has gradually increased from 10% in 1981, and was 13%

in 1991. The proportion of women who were first offenders in 1981 was 18% and this has increased dramatically over the years to 30% in 1991. The differences and trends hold true over all age groups.

Detailed tables showing the relationship between previous criminal history and current offence are provided on an age basis for all offenders, but unfortunately are not broken down by gender, so we cannot say from these whether the high proportion of female first offenders had committed serious offences. However, among persons aged 21 and over who commenced an order (this group has a higher proportion of women) 36% of the first offenders had an offence of theft or handling stolen goods, with a further 16% having an offence of fraud or forgery—the offence groups within which women are most highly represented. I would concur with the recommendation of HM Inspectorate of Probation in their Report on 'Women Offenders and Probation Service Provision' that the Home Office break down more of the tables in Probation Statistics on a gender basis.

Community service orders on women are generally shorter than those on men, which is perhaps not surprising in view of their less serious criminal history, and this has remained true over time. The lengths of orders have gradually become shorter for all offenders, but whilst the difference in the proportion of first offenders has been *increasing*, the difference in the proportion of short orders has been *decreasing*. In 1981 females were much more likely to have orders of less than 150 hours: 68% compared with 55% for men. By 1991 the corresponding figures were 78% of female orders of less than 100 hours compared with 70% of male orders: women still get more short orders, but now only slightly more.

There were relatively few women in the samples of community service workers in our National Study of community service orders, despite including all women rather than a random sample. There were 40 women in all, with the numbers ranging from 5 to 11 in the five community service schemes studied. There was a sample of around a hundred cases in each area and women made up between 5% and 8% of the samples. We did not obtain information about criminal history for four of the women so the total effective sample was 36. Very few women had serious previous criminal histories and 11 had no previous convictions—31%: this was slightly more than the national average for that year (1988/89) but not significantly different. Of particular interest here is the difference between the areas. The two areas with the smallest number of women had no first offenders, and the area with the highest number had just two first offenders. The areas with the highest proportion of first offenders overall (18% and 15%) had the highest of female first offenders (38% and 75%). It may be that the areas with the lowest numbers of women on community service actually have greater equality of access to CS as they are better at gatekeeping that provision.

In my paper to a conference about the impact of National Standards for community service, I outlined why I thought it unlikely that they would lead to more consistent sentencing. I used the relationship between previous criminal history and current offence to (a) highlight the considerable amount of consistency that already existed about the core group of offenders who receive community service, and (b) shed some light on the nature of the inconsistency which occurs. This analysis was based on all offenders together and showed that each area had a significant local pattern of sentencing around the 'margins'.

Without going into all of the detail of the method (which can be obtained from the paper), the two elements of the Cambridgeshire Offender Gravity Rating were used. The criminal history of the offender was rated between 0 and 12, and the current offence was rated between 1 and 5. Each of these scores was grouped into 3 bands: criminal history had 0 to 1, 2 to 8 and 9 to 12; and offence gravity had 1, 2 to 3, and 4 to 5. A matrix with 9 cells was created from these two items of data: the one below shows how the women on whom we had information were distributed and how they compared with the distribution of all community service orders in the study: see *Table 5*.

The results for males and females combined in all the areas show a large degree of consensus with two thirds of the sample falling into the middle cell of the table, ie they were offenders convicted of mid range offences with a mid range criminal history. There was little use of community service for low gravity current offences, particularly for first and second offenders, and no use of community service for offenders with the highest criminal history scores who had committed the most serious offences. This pattern was common to each of the areas in the study. Interesting variations occurred between the areas as to where their marginal orders fell. One area had hardly any orders in the margins, with 84% of all orders falling in the middle group, whilst another had 20% of its cases falling in the low previous history, mid-range offence category. Yet another area had a high proportion of offenders (13%) who were given community service for a relatively minor offence in the mid range criminal history group.

The above analysis shows that there is less consistency overall for women offenders, with only half of the cases falling into the middle group. Most of these cases came from the areas with few first offenders. The areas which had a high proportion of first offenders obviously had more cases in the low criminal history column, but there was no readily identifiable pattern here. Although the numbers in the sample are small, and thus should be treated with caution, my general conclusion is that there is less consensus for female offenders on community service, which suggests that factors other than offence and previous criminal history played a greater part in their sentencing than it did for male offenders.

The role of social inquiry reports

Much of the research addressing issues of sentencing has looked at the role of social inquiry reports (SIRs—now pre-sentence reports). Community service is no exception. Research which I undertook in the early days of community service showed that the nature of the recommendation for community service was an important determinant of whether a community service order was made or not. The influence of the recommendations in general was assessed in a study involving magistrates two years later, when we were able to show that recommendations did indeed yield an influence.

Table 5

OFFENCE GRAVITY RAVING	CRIMINAL HISTORY SCORE					
	0 – 1		2 – 8		9 – 12	
	Female Only	Males & Females	Female Only	Males & Females	Female Only	Males & Females
1		1%	2(6%)	5%	1(3%)	1%
2 – 3	5(14%)	8%	18(50%)	68%	1(3%)	10%
4 – 5	5(14%)	3%	2(6%)	4%	0%	0%

Source: National Study of Community Service Orders, University of Birmingham

70

Jackson and Smith obtained similar results when they compared the social inquiry reports of two samples of women who had been convicted of theft offences: one group had been given a custodial sentence of up to three months and the other had been sentenced to community service. They found that the two groups of women were similar in most respects, but the reports prepared on them were very different. Community service was proposed as an option in 54% of the custodial sentences and 79% of the CSO sentences (the report includes some interesting examples of recommendations from each of the samples). From comparing the two groups of reports, the authors concluded:

'The general tenor and language of the SIRs did, however, seem to be much more positive both about the offenders themselves and about the possibility of community service than the SIRs prepared for the prison sample. So too, was there a tendency for the recommendations for community service in the CSO sample to be more positive and precise.'

This work also found that many of the women in the custody sample had an SIR which contained arguments *against* community service, with the most frequently given reason being the 'domestic responsibilities of the woman as carer'. This ties in with the work of Lena Dominelli who interviewed magistrates, probation officers and community service staff about their 'perceptions of penal processes and female offenders on CS'. She found that women's domestic responsibilities played a complex role in these perceptions, and that women with domestic responsibilities were considered:

'. . . poor risks in relation to community service's organisational objective of getting offenders to complete their orders.'

Recent work by HM Inspectorate of Probation found that on the whole community service staff had a much more positive approach to women on community service than that found by Dominelli in 1984, particularly in relation to any domestic responsibilities they may have. Child minding and creche facilities were often available but not taken up because the CS staff felt that probation officers were not referring these women to be considered for CS. These views were confirmed by the inspectors' reading of reports on women who had been given a custodial sentence. Several reports referred to community service being unsuitable for the woman because of her need to care for small children. This occurred in some areas where arrangements could have been made to look after the children!

Much of the work looking at custodial sentencing has found that women receive custodial sentences earlier in their criminal career than do men, and often for less serious offences. Fewer of them have experienced community service. This is well demonstrated by looking at the sample of 39 women offenders interviewed by Pat Carlen. Thirty seven had served a custodial sentence, 24 had experienced probation or supervision at some time, and yet only two had ever been sentenced to community service. Interestingly, neither of these two women had been subject to probation or supervision. From her discussions with the women, Carlen suggests that personal choice may have a role to play in this as:

71

'. . . dislike of general surveillance had resulted in some going to prison rather than agreeing to probation or community service orders.'

The impact of the Criminal Justice Act 1991
The Criminal Justice Act 1991 aimed to establish greater consistency in sentencing. The Act contained a new statutory framework for sentencing offenders, with proportionality being the guiding criterion for deciding sentence. Section 95 of the Act also contains provisions requiring the Secretary of State to publish annually information to enable those involved in the administration of justice to avoid discrimination on grounds of race, sex or other improper ground. The Act altered the way courts could use community service in several ways. Firstly, it allowed sentencers to combine a community service order with other sentences for a single offence; secondly, it required the court to consider a pre-sentence report before making an order; thirdly, the maximum number of hours was increased for 16 year olds; and finally, the Act made it clear that community service was a sentence in its own right and provided that the offence was serious enough to warrant a community sentence. The Act also introduced the new disposal of a combination order, which is a probation order and a community service order combined.

The Home Office did not anticipate an increase in community service orders would arise from the implementation in the 1991 Act. Correspondence from the Home Office to the Association of Chief Officers of Probation outlined the resource implications of the Act, identifying three proposals with significant resource implications: an increase in the number of pre-sentence reports prepared, especially for the Crown Court; a gradual take up of the new combination order; and additional post-release supervision of offenders. Some allowance was made for additional breach work in probation orders arising from the introduction of National Standards. There was nothing in these resource estimates specifically for improving equality of opportunity, and as Tracey said in his recent paper:

' . . .with bids for scarce resources in the criminal justice system, women may continue to have a low priority.'

It is far too early for any national figures to be available about the impact of the Criminal Justice Act on sentencing, and in particular to assess its impact on the sentencing of women offenders. Work undertaken in local probation services is attesting to a significant change in sentencing patterns in both magistrates' courts and the Crown Court, and in particular highlighting a huge increase in the number of community service orders made, an increase which as we have seen was not anticipated by the Home Office.

This increase in community service overall might be positive for women if it has increased their access to the disposal. Examination of the impact of the Criminal Justice Act in courts in Derbyshire in relation to women and community service has yielded the results presented in *Table 6*. Some results are encouraging, others not so. I am very grateful to Derbyshire Probation Service for allowing the publication of these figures. I must emphasise that the results presented here are provisional and based on local data only. This picture may not hold true for the rest of the country, but the analysis throws some very useful first light on the subject, and highlights the sort of analysis which needs to be done at a national level to address the question.

Table 6 shows that Derbyshire has experienced an increase overall in the number of pre-sentence reports, but the increase has been much greater for males than for females. The proportion of reports which were prepared for the Crown Court has also gone up for both males and females, and here the increase is actually greater for women than for men. This may be because women are more likely to have their cases dealt with by the Crown Court, or it could be that more women had been dealt with without a report in the nine months prior to the introduction of the Act. Reports on both women and men have been more likely to contain a proposal for community service since the introduction of the Act, but it is still much more likely that reports on men will contain such a proposal than reports on women. Courts have been less likely to agree with a proposal for community service for women than they did prior to the Act, whereas they have been much more likely to agree with such a proposal for men. The net result is that, proportionately, there has been an increase in reports on both men and women which result in a community service sentence, but the increase has been much more for men than it has for women. This in effect means that women are in a less equal position with men than they were, despite their likelihood of a community service order increasing.

Looking at the sentences of community service which have been made, we can see that the number of sentences of community service for women increased by 30%, but the increase in sentences for men was 37% (a huge increase which is creating many difficulties). More important for the purposes of this analysis is an examination of the nature of those sentences and whether they vary for males and females. The previous criminal history of those people who were sentenced to community service is less serious than it was: for both men and women the mean number of previous convictions has gone down, and the proportion of first offenders has increased. The increase in female offenders is particularly noticeable. A look at the actual type of offence for which the community service order was given demonstrates the different pattern for men and women: this has remained consistent for men but has changed considerably for women in the nine months since the implementation of the Act. It may be that with the numbers of women being relatively small there has been some local incident which has skewed the figures, but it is interesting that there is an increase in property offences and a decrease in violence. This area needs a closer examination of the data. We cannot tell from the offence category just how serious the offences might have been, and what the aggravating and mitigating features may have been in these cases. Some tentative work Derbyshire has been carrying out on scoring seriousness indicates that there is no big difference in seriousness levels between the men and women who were sentenced to community service, and that there has been no real change over time.

Table 6

Sentences of Community Service

Number of CS sentences	30	39	478	653
Mean number previous convictions	2.8	1.7	5.3	4.3
% first offenders	27%	49%	15%	20%
% theft offences	33%	39%	18%	16%
% fraud offences	7%	28%	4%	4%
% violence offences	30%	8%	17%	17%
% with proposal for community service	47%	44%	58%	67%
% with proposal for conditional discharge	23%	26%	13%	7%
Average order length	90.2	106.5	116.0	121.3
% with order length 40 – 100 hours	73%	62%	48%	44%
% aged 17 – 20	30%	15%	37%	28%

Based on Derbyshire offence seriousness classification 01 – 12
Source: Derbyshire Probation Service Report Monitoring System

Table 6 Pre–sentence reports prepared by Derbyshire probation officers January – September 1992 and October 1992 – June 1993

Females		All Reports	Males	
Pre CJA	Post CJA		Pre CJA	Post CJA
193	196	Total number of reports	1867	1936
33%	18%	% reports for Crown Court	39%	22%
13%	18%	% proposals for CS	27%	35%
54%	49%	% proposals for Cs with sentences of CS	55%	64%
16%	20%	% sentences of CS	26%	34%

The evidence of lesser previous criminal histories and no significant change in offence would have led us to expect a decrease in order length if any change in length was to occur, but the opposite has actually happened. Order lengths have increased for both women and men, but the increase in lengths of women's orders is the greater. Having said this, the orders made on women are still generally shorter than those made on men, with almost two-thirds being of 100 hours or less in the last nine months.

The conclusions for Derbyshire Probation Service are that there are more women being given community service orders than there were, but that these additional orders share characteristics of the 'lower tariff' males who are given community service. Average lengths of orders are getting longer, which seems to indicate that local application by courts of the test 'commensurate with the seriousness of the offence' has led to longer orders than was previously the case. The comparison with males is particularly difficult as their position with regard to community service has moved in ways we would not have wished. Overall then, there is no evidence in Derbyshire that the Criminal Justice Act 1991 has improved access to community service for women, and some evidence that access has deteriorated. Derbyshire is an area with a very high use of community service by courts, but there is no reason to believe that features in this county are radically different from elsewhere in the country. We will thus await comparative results from the rest of the country with interest.

Conclusion

As with much analysis, we end up in a position of knowing quite a lot about our area of enquiry, but feeling the need to know more before we can draw any positive conclusions. I feel the area where we particularly need more work is an examination of the disparity in sentencing between different courts. Barbara Hudson, discussing issues of race, says that we need to look more closely at the combined effect of discrimination and disparity. This point applies equally to issues of gender.

The majority of offenders are young, white and male. Offenders are dealt with by a criminal justice system which, though gradually changing, is still a predominantly white, male, middle-class institution. Because of this, most of the work looking at the place of women in the criminal justice system has aimed at making women's position the same as that of men. Alison Young, in a paper to the British Criminology Conference in 1991, presents a critique of the traditional 'equality' model whereby the male majority is used as the lynchpin for analysis, against which minority groups are compared.

'If like is to be treated alike, then men and women should receive the same treatment. However men are employed as the standard for comparison; thus, Woman's subordination to Man is reiterated by the emphasis on equality.'

Such an approach implies that inequality is only important when a minority is disadvantaged, when in fact it may be the majority which is disadvantaged. Rob Waters in his work on race has suggested that inequality may be an indication that something positive is happening, something which we may want to encourage. He suggests that the lower rates of proposals for probation orders for black offenders is the result of probation officers responding positively to the preferences expressed by the offender during the preparation of a report. This approach is worthy of consideration, for as the National Study of Community Service has suggested, it is quite possible that the low numbers of women given a community service order is a positive finding.

The outcome of all this analysis, then, is something of a conundrum. There is no evidence from the matched sample studies to suggest that women and men in similar circumstances are sentenced differently, yet we know that there is a much higher proportion of first offender women on community service who have committed relatively minor offences than men. At the same time studies of people in custody again show that women in custody have less serious criminal histories and have committed less serious offences than have men. The problem of access appears to be not a simple one of how to increase the number of women on community service, but how to ensure that the women who are given community service are not being sentenced more severely than men would be in the same position. That requires a shift of the sentencing of women offenders 'up-tariff', such that the 'low-tariff' women who currently receive community service orders are given less intrusive sentences, more commensurate with the seriousness of the offence, and that many of the women who are currently given a custodial sentence are instead sentenced to community service.

Access for women then is not particularly friendly. It is too flexible in some ways, drawing in many 'low tariff' women, yet not flexible enough in others, excluding women with maybe difficult circumstances. What is needed is some friendly persuasion, demonstrating that women in a range of circumstances can and do successfully complete community service orders. We have to persuade women that community service would be a worthwhile option for them; persuade more probation officers to refer women for community service, even where they think their domestic circumstances might be problematic; and persuade courts that community service is a viable sentencing option for (appropriate) women with a range of domestic circumstances. Easy to say, but not so easy to do!

REFERENCES

Allen H (1987) *The logic of gender in psychiatric reports to the courts.* In Pennington D C and Lloyd-Bostock S (eds), 'The Psychology of Sentencing'. Oxford: Centre for Socio-Legal Studies

Carlen P (1988) *Women, Crime and Poverty.* Open University Press, Milton Keynes

Dominelli L (1984) *Differential Justice: Domestic Labour, Community Service and Female Offenders.* Probation Journal vol 38, no 3

HM Inspectorate of Probation (1991) *Report on Women Offenders and Probation Service Provision: Report of a Thematic Inspection.* HM Inspectorate of Probation, London

Hine J, McWilliams W and Keith D (1976) *Recommendations and Community Service*. South Yorkshire Probation Service. Unpublished discussion paper

Hine J, McWilliams W and Pease K (1978) *Recommendations, Social Information and Sentencing*. Howard Journal, vol 17, no 2

Hine J (1991) *Standards and Sentencing: a Magical Mystery Tour*. Paper presented to conference 'Community Service Orders: the Impact of National Standards', Nottingham Polytechnic, September 1991

Home Office (1989) *Criminal and Custodial Careers of those born 1953, 1958 and 1963*. Statistical Bulletin 32/89, HMSO, London

Home Office (1992) *Statistics on Community Service*. Statistical Bulletin 13/92, HMSO, London

Home Office (1992) *Gender and the Criminal Justice System*. HMSO, London

Home Office (1993) *Probation Statistics England & Wales 1991*. HMSO, London

Home Office (1993) *Criminal Statistics: England & Wales 1991*. Home Office, London

Home Office (1993) *Summary Probation Statistics England & Wales 1992*. Statistical Bulletin 17/93, HMSO, London

Hudson B (1989) *Discrimination and disparity: researching the influence of race on sentencing*. Paper given to British Criminology Conference 1989

Jackson H and Smith L (1987) *Female Offenders: an analysis of SIRs*. Home Office Research Bulletin No 23, HMSO, London

Mair G and Brockington N (1988) *Female Offenders and the Probation Service*. Howard Journal, vol 27

Moxon D (1988) *Sentencing Practice in the Crown Court*. Home Office Research Study No103, Home Office, London

Ramsay M (1984) *Women and Crime: a Changing Pattern of Convictions*. Home Office Research Bulletin No 17, HMSO, London

Thomas, Hine and Nugent (1990) *Study of Community Service Orders: Summary Report*. Unpublished report to the Home Office

Tracey J (1992) *Women in the Criminal Justice System*. Justice of the Peace, vol 156, 11 July 1992

Wasik M and Taylor RD (1991) *Blackstone's Guide to the Criminal Justice Act 1991*. Blackstone's, London

Waters R (1988) *Race and the Criminal Justice Process*. British Journal of Criminology, vol 28, no 1

Worrall A (1981) *Out of place: Female Offenders in Court*. Probation Journal, vol 36

Young A (1991) *Feminism and the Body of Criminology*. Paper given to British Criminology Conference July 1991

'All aboard!'. On the right track in Merseyside

Before

. . . and after

Darenth Park Riding School for the Disabled, Kent

Designed and built after hours. Adventure playground, Crawley, West Sussex

'Firm but fair'. The pivotal role of the community service officer

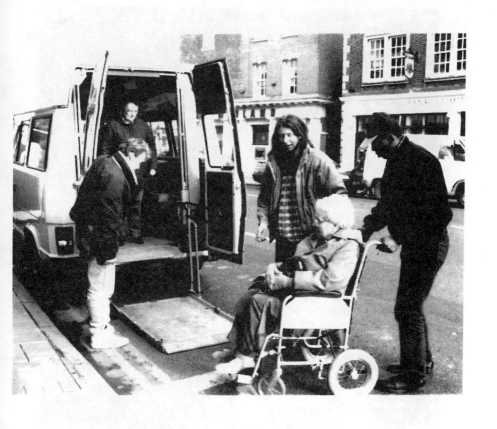

'Without community service we wouldn't get out at all'.
Wheelchair shopping, Wiltshire

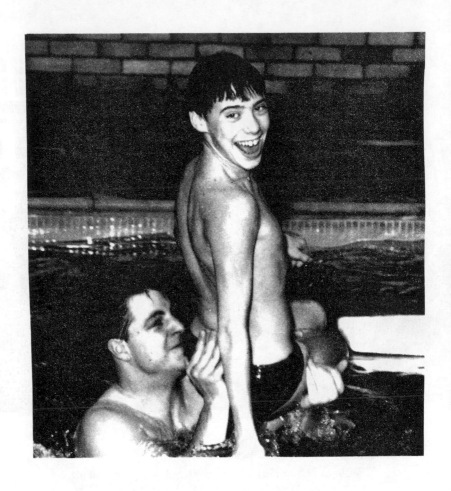

A helping hand. Community service in Wiltshire

'At your service'. A luncheon club in Sheffield

'Something like this is so worthwhile'.
A cot built by the Wirral Community Service Unit

'Extending the boundaries'. Surrey CS at work in Deva Children's Hospital

Extending the boundaries with Viorel Scornea who became
a mascot for the CS team in Rumania

Chapter 6 Extending the Boundaries

Dick Whitfield

One of the hallmarks of community service has been its determined refusal to stand still. This chapter looks at the way the boundaries have been extended in all kinds of ways—more varied and more creative placements; wider acceptance by the public, for whom community service is often the most visible of the activities undertaken by the probation service; a much wider range of offenders placed on orders as confidence in the scheme grew; a rapid growth, internationally and, finally, an English scheme which also extended to include an international project.

But how is it that such change and diversity could have been achieved in a relatively short time? Part of the reason may lie in the varied range of people who were recruited to run many of the community service schemes in this country, either alongside probation officers or on their own. I recently asked an independent management consultant to review aspects of the scheme in Kent, where the operation is devolved to local offices, most of which have a single community service officer. He described the overall effect as 'like a series of one-man businesses, with all the entrepreneurial benefits and responsiveness you would expect—and with the same characteristic tendencies, too, of always pushing onward and outward.' Keeping a lively, responsive and un-bureaucratic operation while still working to consistent standards is one of the keys to continued growth and the upsurge in orders which has followed the Criminal Justice Act 1991 has made achieving that balance an urgent task, too.

Yet the starting point was tentative, to say the least.

Detailed planning for community service was undertaken by a Home Office working group whose report (1) not only set many of the ground rules but also revealed the limits within which they thought the scheme might operate. The group consulted widely with local authorities and with voluntary organisations before publishing a list of tasks which, it said, fell broadly into two categories—work of a practical nature not involving personal relationships with clients and, secondly, tasks involving relationships with beneficiaries to a greater or lesser extent. The two groups were listed more fully in an appendix to the report, as follows:

i) cleaning rubbish not dealt with by ordinary refuse disposal or street cleaning
ii) cleaning footpaths, helping in nature reserves
iii) reclamation work on slag heaps and similar eyesores
iv) decorating houses for occupation by fatherless or otherwise deprived

families, and
v) constructing adventure playgrounds.

Tasks involving personal relationships were listed as:

i) decorating or gardening for old or disabled people
ii) acting as drivers or attendants to handicapped children, the old, or disabled
iii) assisting in geriatric and mental hospitals with a variety of tasks, and
iv) supervising adventure playground activities, running football teams.

The working group made it clear that they had doubts about how extensively the scheme might be used by courts and they also felt that community service might be constrained by the availability of work from local authorities, who they thought, were bound to be the main source of placements.

'Some authorities think there would be a regular supply of unskilled labouring work . . . although others can give no assurance that work would be available at a given time.' (2)

Not surprisingly, other doubts were surfacing, too. Would any scheme which used voluntary bodies compromise the character and philosophy of voluntary service—and would any scheme of a punitive nature compromise the traditional image of the probation service as a helping and treating agency? Would community service prove to be feasible in areas of high unemployment? Would the participation of offenders in local authority projects have a detrimental effect on bonus schemes? And what would the attitude of the trade unions be? The working group thought that the only way these hazards might be addressed was to start with a few pilot areas, and while they retained their opinion about this 'new and potentially creative' option for the courts it is doubtful if they had any idea of how swiftly and how extensively it would flower.

By way of comparison with the Home Office task list the report on one of the experimental areas, Nottinghamshire, lists the tasks undertaken during its first year of operation (3). There are thirty of them and all the tasks listed by the Home Office had already been covered. But the boundaries were also being extended and the report lists

—helping to run a community newspaper
—work in day centres for the elderly
—work with the local Ambulance Service
and helping road safety organisations, among many others.

Nor were local authority departments the main providers of work. John Harding, the organiser, was clear about the reason: 'The voluntary organisations in Nottinghamshire were initially more accessible than their local authority counterparts since effective decision making often lay in the hands of a few people at the heart of the organisation' (4). Sixty-five per cent of all community service work was undertaken through single placements with voluntary organisations in these early stages—a very different picture to the one expected. And one boundary, it was clear, was already being tested. 'In asking community groups to accept and involve offenders as helpers we are pushing back the conventional stereotypes of offenders and widening the threshold of tolerance. In that process we are, perhaps, asking the community to grow with us'. (5)

By the ten year mark a report on community service aimed specifically at sentencers (6) was accepting a wide variety of placements as normal and was more concerned with the difference of approach and standards around the country. Quoting Richards and Maull (7) it noted—

'in some cases, offenders on community service sweat their way to redemption through the punishing self-mortification of hard work. In others, a 'treatment' model applies, with caring supervisors, carefully chosen placements, offender support and occasional casework intervention'.

There was no doubt which approach was preferred. The report gives particular examples of what it considered best practice, especially the range of schemes developed in Wiltshire which included

—a 'Saturday Club' for mentally handicapped children, in which two supervisors and 12 community service workers not only cared for the children but gave their normal carers a precious day off
—a wheelchair shopping service for the elderly and disabled
—a hospital visiting service
—a 'Helping Hand' scheme to provide practical assistance to individuals and families in crisis.

It would be difficult to over-emphasise the impact which the Wiltshire projects had on community service nationally and many similar schemes are now in operation. As the organisers noted, 'a service of this type has no inherent terminal date and the demand for it is potentially inexhaustible'.

Other schemes to catch the eye were three run by Greater Manchester Probation Service; a 'soup run' for down and outs in the city centre and dockland areas, work at city hostels for travellers and involvement in a large Youth Club where offenders worked alongside the police in providing sports and recreational facilities. But even a cursory glance at the annual reports of area probation services revealed that, along with the increase in numbers, the whole range of placements by the early 1980's was considerable and impressive. Large scale conservation and environmental schemes provided work for quite large groups for long periods of time and became popular with organisers who had to cope with fluctuating numbers; improvements to local community facilities such as adventure playgrounds, village halls, churchyards, schools and community centres also seemed to be endless. A growing number of schemes also concentrated on help to voluntary organisations such as Age Concern, the Salvation Army, and charities concerned with everything from help to patients with head injuries to the Riding for the Disabled scheme. And while all this was going on, community service was also making a real impact abroad.

Interest from other countries followed the English launch very swiftly and even before the experimental phase had been completed it was clear that both the simplicity of the scheme and its apparent effectiveness had commended it to politicians and criminal justice personnel alike. Although its legislative status varies considerably from country to country—it can be imposed by a prosecutor as a condition of non-prosecution; as part of a conditional sentence of imprisonment; as a direct alternative to custody or as a suspended sentence which includes a duty to do unpaid work in the public interest during leisure hours—the similarities in practice show just how rapid the spread has been.

Using Europe as an example, *Table 1* gives an outline chronology. (8)

Table 1

YEAR INTRODUCED	COUNTRY	COMMENT
1973	England & Wales	Five experimental areas
1974	Switzerland	Juveniles only
1975	Federal Republic of Germany	Also used as penalty for fine default
1976	Luxembourg	
1981	Italy	"Substitute labour" – alternative to fine
1981	Netherlands	Pilot project (national:1986)
1982	Belgium	Juveniles only
1982	Denmark	Pilot project (national:1984)
1982	Portugal	
1983	France	
1984	Ireland	
1984	Norway	Pilot project (national:1989)
1992	Sweden	

Exactly how different its development has been is best demonstrated by several examples.

In DENMARK the legal basis of the original experiment, which covered two regions, one of which was the city of Copenhagen, is the penal code section and rules on suspended sentences. Courts may stipulate special conditions according to the needs of the individual offender when considering a suspended sentence and one of these is a specified period of unpaid work for the community (from 40 to 200 hours) which must be completed within a set period (generally 4 to 12 months depending on the number of hours ordered).

Such an order can be suggested by the court itself, the public prosecutor, defence counsel or the probation officer but it can only be made if certain criteria are met. The first of these is the intended 'target group'—initially young offenders whose conviction for a property offence would normally attract a sentence of 6 to 8 months imprisonment, although other types and ages of offenders can now be included. The second is the characteristics of the offender; there is an understandable reluctance to use community service for those with substantial drug or alcohol problems, or the mentally ill.

The probation service organises all the necessary work placements, most of which are for one person only. Supervision of these 'singleton' placements is by someone already engaged there, with regular spot checks by the Probation Department and, typically, work is concentrated on public and non-profit making institutions or those which use only voluntary labour. A 'Labour Market Committee', on which the Trade Unions are represented, oversees the scheme to ensure that community service workers do not take over jobs which should be reserved for paid labour.

Breach proceedings, usually instituted for non attendance, occur in about 17% of cases and generally mean that the suspended prison sentence is brought into effect.

In complete contrast, in ITALY, community service is intended to act as a substitute for a fine. Provided that the original fine is no more than 1,000,000 lire (£440), up to 60 days may be worked by the offender, with 50,000 lire (£22) credited for each complete day worked. Usually, the offender is limited to one day's work per week. Only very limited experimentation has taken place so far, although the legal framework has been in place since 1981, and there is still the possibility that community service could be introduced as a penalty in its own right.

In HOLLAND it was the Committee on Alternative Penal Sanctions, in tackling the task of trying to reduce the use of short unconditional prison sentences, which promoted the use of the community service order. They set a clear framework for such orders (which were originally for a maximum of 50 hours) and insisted that work had to meet the following requirements:

i) it had to provide a significant social service (for instance projects in the public health sector or environment or projects of an educational or recreational nature);
ii) it had to be undertaken in conjunction with volunteers from the community—there were to be no 'offender-only' groups;

iii) work had to be undertaken in 'normal' free time, and in the offender's own locality.

Once these had been established, however, the Dutch set about adapting the community service scheme to fit in with their usual approach to crime. Community service work is thus possible within a framework of non-prosecution, postponement of the decision to prosecute, conditional non-prosecution and deferment of sentence. Agreement from the offender is required; the scheme is intended as a direct alternative to a short (up to six months) prison sentence. The success of the new initiative can be gauged from the numbers of orders made which increased by three thousand per cent over a decade. (9)

1981	-	213
1982	-	917
1984	-	2431
1986	-	3419
1988	-	4913
1990	-	6626

During 1990/91 a number of community service staff from Kent and from other south eastern probation areas undertook an exchange scheme with their counterparts in both Holland and (what was then) West Germany. In addition to learning about the structural and legal differences between schemes there were opportunities to compare projects and it soon became clear to Kent staff that the overwhelming majority of single placements, rather than group projects, was the hallmark of the Dutch scheme. One participant, Sarah Adelsberg, was based in Leeuwarden, which had four community service officers and a regional officer—and 240 individual project placements on which they could draw. She wrote:

'All work carried out by the offenders is by arrangement with the chosen project and is supervised by them. Local councils have quite an input and have no objection to providing work—for example at a swimming pool or leisure centre. Local unemployed people are also placed at these projects. Where possible, the worker is 'matched' to the project and this takes place at the initial interview stage. Then an interview is arranged at the agency for the offender/worker, and the community service officer. Working days and hours of work are arranged and a starting date set. The offender can work as many hours and days as are suitable to the project. On one project I visited he was working from 9.00 to 5.00, Monday to Friday. All the community service workers I spoke to preferred to work in blocks and felt a sense of continuity. Some were in full time employment and were doing their community service hours in their holiday from work.'

The emphasis seems to be on getting the work completed as effectively as possible. In England and Wales, there is a maximum figure of 21 hours per week which is allowable and it may be that this could be reviewed when National Standards are reconsidered in 1994.

In Leeuwarden there was only one group project, providing communal facilities for a housing association, and this was reserved for offenders who were reckoned to be 'difficult to place' in individual projects. The difficulties may relate to behaviour, seriousness of offence or perceived risk—but the group was only experimental and there is no doubt that Dutch staff saw individual placements as the main objective. They are very flexible in terms of hours worked, provide for a wide range of skills (or produce very simple but necessary tasks for the unskilled) and are cheap to run. The receiving agency provides supervision, notes the hours worked and forwards a weekly return and the community service officer only visits if there are problems. The model may be different, but community service is as well established in a decade, in the Netherlands, as it is here.

I have concentrated on European experience to make a simple point: that the spread of community service has been varied, but has also been rapid and widespread. Examples could just as easily have been drawn from Australasia, the Far East or North America—at a recent United Nations Crime Commission meeting an impromptu survey suggested that the sentence—or an adaptation of it—is now available in over 40 countries, and the list has additions to it almost every year. In terms of growth it has been the centrepiece of community based sanctions and has earned that position in a comparatively short time.

Looking abroad, however, does more than just emphasise that steady and sometimes spectacular growth. It also demonstrates, on occasion, where the boundaries have been stretched to the limit, and sometimes to breaking point. Inevitably, examples are most easily found in the USA.

Community service was not, in any case, a wholly English invention. The notion of using the offender as a community resource was not in itself new when the Wootton Committee reported in 1970, since scattered experiments had been taking place on both sides of the Atlantic, especially in the late 1960's and in the year or two before 1973, when the English experiment began.

Probably the most significant of the experimental programmes was started in New York by the Vera Institute of Justice (so often at the cutting edge of criminal justice development) in 1972. Set against the background of hopelessly overextended probation caseloads and a burgeoning prison population, the new community service programme soon had 1200 'jail bound recidivists' as the search for new, effective intermediate sanctions began. Eligibility criteria specified that those admitted to the Vera programme must be multiple offenders and have prior convictions. Soon, initiatives were under way across the nation; in 1976 the National Institute of Law Enforcement and Criminal Justice made $1.6 million in grants available for community service and restitution programmes in seven states and two years later the Office of Juvenile Justice and Delinquency Prevention provided $30 million for 85 further programmes. All too often, however, community service has been used as an add-on to a probation order and has simply become part of the net-widening process. Todd Clear and George Cole (10), surveying the experience of a decade and a half, wrote:

'Community service has recently become very popular. The idea is powerfully attractive; the person convicted of a crime serves the community in some public manner, thereby overcoming some of the harm caused by the crime. Community service has an advantage over fines in that even indigent offenders can perform some work. There is also symbolic value in the offender's effort to make reparation to the community. The popularity of community service has made it vulnerable to over use as an add-on to probation terms, making it merely an enhanced form of probation, not a true alternative to incarceration.'

Clear and Cole also found the evidence of effectiveness rather mixed and added: 'No final verdict has been reached on the value of community service as an alternative to jail.' Comparisons are, in fact, very difficult to make when high-profile cases may involve community service of well over one thousand hours, even though the average is just under 100 hours. The problem was simply put:

'The problem is one of scale. When the penal code's normal punishment for an offence is incarceration then such sanctions as . . . community service seem pallid by comparison and are imposed only as a 'second chance' rather than as a direct punishment for a crime. When everyone placed on probation is given a community service sentence and a fine as well, each of these sanctions loses some of its punitive impact and symbolic value. The time has come to recognise two crucial facts:

1. The United States hands out punitive sanctions far in excess of those imposed by most other Western democracies
2. We have under correctional supervision a far larger proportion of our citizenry than any other comparable nation.' (11)

They might have added that the search for ways of managing this over-supervised citizenry would also extend the boundaries in ways which are now of particular interest in this country. It was in the USA that 'contracting out' of entire community service schemes was first undertaken and a recent report (12) looks at the experience of two such schemes. This is Mary Fielder's description of community service arrangements in Los Angeles:

'The vast majority of defendants ordered to perform CS in the Los Angeles Courts are directed to organizations known as 'Volunteer Centres'. Volunteer Centres are the traditional brokers between persons who wish to volunteer their time, and community organizations which need volunteers to carry out their goals. Assisting the Courts in placing defendants on community service is just one part of this overall function. Payment is made to the Volunteer Centre by the Probation Department based on the number of defendants served by the Centre in the preceding year. The largest Centre dealt with 29,000 defendants in 1988/89, and the smallest just over 600.

Once made subject of CS Order, the offender is instructed to make contact with a Volunteer Centre and may go to any centre of their choosing. The Court specifies the number of hours to be worked, and the date by which the order must be completed. The Court may also specify the nature of the work to be undertaken. A date is set for the defendant to return to Court, when he/she will be required to demonstrate that the hours ordered have been completed, this being verified by report from the Centre. Work assignments may be with a variety of non-profit making organizations, and extensive use is made of placements with California Department of Transportation on litter clearing tasks. The Volunteer Centre arranges the work, but does not undertake any direct supervision of work assignments, nor does it pursue any failures to attend. The responsibility is placed entirely on the offender, who must ultimately answer to the Court for any non-compliance.

Each Volunteer Centre is also permitted, under the terms of its contract to charge defendants a fee, to defray the Centre's actual operating expenses. The fee charged varies with the hours ordered, the range being $5 to $40. The Court has the power to waive the fee, due to 'indigency'.

The Probation Department also organizes the 'Probation Adult Alternative Work Service'. Probationers convicted of minor offences can be ordered to undertake 30 days full time work, as an alternative to spending time in custody. A variety of other Court ordered work schemes are run variously by the Volunteer Centres, other community organizations, the Clerk to the Court Administrator, and the Sheriff's Department. There is also some overlap with the Work Furlough Programme supervised by the Probation Department, which allows sentenced prisoners to leave the custodial facility during specified hours to pursue normal employment or education. Community Service may also be a condition of an inmate's release on Parole from a County jail, although in practice is seldom imposed.'

Different groups, of course, had different views about the advantages and disadvantages of 'contracting out'. Government officials thought that it helped to achieve change more quickly; overcame the usual resistance to expansion in the public sector, was cost-effective and actually encouraged real community action. Their belief was that using public finance helped to develop small, local innovative schemes. Difficulties were also acknowledged—of cancelling contracts (especially to non-profit groups who have political and community support), and of monitoring and evaluating local schemes—but they were felt to be minor in comparison to the advantages.

For Chief Probation Officers the balance was somewhat different. They were concerned about the insecurity of contracts placed with other bodies; the inconsistency of service which often followed and the danger of unscrupulous profiteering by some private operators. The most spectacular example of the first of these was in Harris County, Texas, when the private contract agency responsible for community service schemes, Community Service Option Programme, simply closed its doors and ceased operating. This unplanned occurrence left the Probation Department with immediate responsibility for 4000 outstanding orders—and no staff or organisational structure to deal with it. It took just over a year before the new, in-house, community service unit became fully functional and gave probation departments across the USA a good deal of food for thought about the wisdom of placing large, essential services in private hands.

• • • • •

Perhaps the most significant—and dramatic—extension of boundaries in community service has been provided by the Surrey Probation Service's Romanian project. The idea of taking a group of community service workers to Romania grew from a conversation between the Chief Probation Officer, Michael Varah and a local journalist (an ex-probation officer) who had just returned from Romania in the Autumn of 1990. It developed into a partnership with a local Community Church and the Surrey Care Trust and by Easter 1991 the first project was under way—an impressive feat in itself, given the enormous logistical and planning problems.

The project had two main aims: to provide a modest amount of humanitarian aid to a country whose needs were urgent and overwhelming and to provide a unique work programme for offenders that would increase their tolerance and sense of responsibility and reduce their offending behaviour. The church group who were to become partners in the enterprise had already established links with a large orphanage for 500 children in the town of Deva, in Central Romania. The initial report proposing the scheme pulled no punches as it described the needs and the work which would have to be undertaken.

'The majority of the children are young but some have remained at the orphanage beyond their teens and are now in their early twenties. A number suffer from mental and/or physical disability. The very young sleep two to a cot, and the older ones four to a bed. The heating system is never adequate and frequently breaks down. Each room is crammed with beds or cots. The mattresses are soiled. The walls have not been painted for many years. There are no decorations or personal effects to be seen. The atmosphere smells of urine. The task for our offenders will be very demanding'. (13)

The project actually undertaken was the total refurbishment of a childrens' hospital with a capacity for 110 youngsters and the organisation would have put off all but the most determined. All materials for redecoration, repairs to electrical and plumbing systems had, of course, to be taken from the UK. So, too, did supplies for the party who had to be completely self sufficient or be an impossible burden to their impoverished hosts. The local press was hostile; the trip was undertaken under intense scrutiny including a Thames Television team and yet the community service team had not only to complete its work—it had to try and encourage and sustain Romanian volunteers to go on helping themselves after the departure of the community service group. There were moments when it seemed unlikely the project would ever get started. Fuelled by adverse press comment, the local authorities in Deva were so terrified of the 'ruthless gangsters' who had appeared that initially, they refused permission for them even to unload their trucks.

Astonishingly, it worked. No one who saw the resulting T.V. documentary programme on the trip (14) could fail to be impressed and moved by the reaction of the young community service workers and the response they achieved from both the children and staff in the orphanage. Work went on for 9 hours a day— far in excess of the actual community service orders, of course—and the sense of working as a team was very apparent as large parts of the dilapidated and depressing orphanage were restored to life.

Even more astonishingly to many, the Surrey Service were later subject to substantial criticism from the Home Office, who complained that community service work abroad could not fulfil the requirement that work should benefit the community offended *against* and that various requirements of the scheme, including maximum hours to be worked in any one week, were being infringed. The Surrey Probation Committee weighed the issues very carefully before deciding to give their full support to subsequent visits and so fulfil the expectations which had been established. In reaching this decision they had considerable support from sentencers, who were very impressed by the project.

On the second visit there were 19 offenders, compared with 11 on the first occasion. A number of changes had been made following the experience of the first trip—air travel instead of a gruelling trip by coach across Europe, better catering facilities were two of the most important—and 45 more rooms and 8 corridors were thoroughly redecorated, replacement light fittings installed and simple plumbing repairs undertaken. The materials and supplies still had to be transported across Europe by lorry, of course, and the partnership with Guildford Community Church remained an essential part of the complex operation which such a large group inevitably entailed. A wide range of businesses and charities provided cash or goods so that the group was not only completely self sufficient—it was able to donate 7000 syringes and hypodermic needles, one ton of orange juice, 100 new blankets and curtains for each childrens ward.

The first trip had demonstrated the extraordinary effect which the whole project had on those who took part—the contact with children (and adults) experiencing a level of deprivation far beyond their own imagining; the sense of hopelessness transformed by their own work, cheerfulness and belief; and the knowledge that they could make a real and valued contribution. It was a potent mix and two of those first eleven who journeyed to Deva later returned voluntarily to Romania to work with a charitable relief agency. Yet the second trip was not without its problems, despite meticulous preparation. The group was carefully chosen, well briefed and had some experience of working together as they undertook the first 21 hours of their orders immediately prior to the trip in a geriatric hospital in Surrey. But two had to be sent home because of disruptive behaviour fuelled by the easy availability of strong cheap local beer and two became involved in a fracas the night before the return trip. This resulted in the local police insisting they paid £40 each towards compensation to avoid prosecution. The pressures of two weeks hard, demanding work were matched by the pressures which surfaced locally, after dark.

The majority of the group, however, responded as positively as expected and indeed the behaviour of almost all of them since the earliest trip has been a tribute to the impact which the experience provided. Only one has re-offended; almost all agree that it has changed completely both their attitude to life and their view of their own values and behaviour. The scheme is most accurately summed up in an extensive newspaper report (15) under the heading, 'Now that really *is* Community Service' and by-lined 'Mission Impossible'.

'The band of British law-breakers are now heroes in Deva, Transylvania where they have sweated for up to 12 hours a day to transform a damp, rundown hospital with its leaking roof and grey, peeling walls.

99

Doctors and nurses watched in awe as they chipped away crumbling plaster, repaired rotting window frames and completely re-wired wards where sockets and light fittings hadn't seen electric current for years.

The hospital's senior paediatrician, Dr Viorica Burda said: "They are so wonderful and kind coming to help us like this. We were afraid when they arrived. Our newspapers said they were killers and rapists and some people thought they were going to be murdered in their beds.

I had been told they had committed offences in England and I was happy so long as they were not dangerous to children. When we read these terrible things in the papers naturally we were very frightened.

But after the police chief told us it was safe we trusted them and now we know what lovely people they are".'

Large-scale community service work abroad may be neither feasible nor desirable but the pioneering work undertaken by Surrey Probation Service has caught the imagination of sentencers and community service staff alike. The aims of community service are practical rather than rehabilitative; to pay back something of value to the community offended against; to reinforce notions of personal responsibility (and, if possible, of personal worth). Yet here is a scheme which goes a good deal further and which has apparently had a positive impact far beyond the expectations of its organisers for, although in personal terms the offenders were carefully chosen, in terms of re-offending they were a high-risk group. The kind of work undertaken, too, was of real and immediate value and the needs, in Romania, in other Eastern European countries and with the prospect of a large scale reconstruction in the former Yugoslavia as well, are almost overwhelming.

This community service project, however, was seen by the Home Office to have extended the boundaries to breaking point and their view that it contravened national standards in terms of working patterns and in not providing locally-based work has not been resolved. Other questions have not yet arisen because of the overwhelming success of the venture but Surrey staff have always been very conscious of the high profile of the scheme—and the high costs of failure, should something go wrong. A single serious offence by a community service worker in Romania might have an impact far beyond the actual behaviour; even minor problems risk an uncertain response from the people and services of a depressed communist regime whose attitude to Western aid is still ambivalent.

Surrey decided that risks were best managed by careful selection of the offender group, by thorough planning and by establishing a disciplined regime throughout the project which was understood and accepted by all who participated. It paid dividends, not just in work achievements but in the rewards of much positive publicity. Following the first project it was noticeable that the number of community service orders made in Surrey courts rose steadily. Sentencers' appreciation of the Romania project was almost certainly a factor in this increase.

The first trip to Romania, with its attendant press and television publicity left many of us with a view that it was an admirable but unique, one-off event that had no real part in the main stream of community service development and was too risky to be repeated. With a more ambitious and equally successful

100

second trip completed and plans for further involvement, that view has to be reconsidered. The project not only exceeds the usual very demanding work requirements of community service, it demonstrates the value of working partnerships with the voluntary sector and provides a quality of experience which seems to have a real impact on offending behaviour. With good management and careful planning, community service has shown that boundaries can still be extended and that the limits of that creativity which the Home Office Planning Group recognised would be vital, have yet to be reached.

REFERENCES

(1) Report from the Working Group on Community Service by Offenders, Home Office, London (1971)

(2) *Ibid,* p 2 para 4

(3) *Community Service by Offenders—the Nottinghamshire experiment.* J Harding (ed), NACRO London 1974

(4) *Ibid,* p 5

(5) *Ibid,* p 18

(6) *Community Service Orders—a guide for sentencers,* Stephen Shaw (1983), London, Prison Reform Trust

(7) *Making Community Service into Service for the Community,* N Richards and G Maull, vol 29, no 3, Probation Journal 1982

(8) Derived from 'Sanctions Systems in Member States of the Council'. Kalmthout and Tak, Kenwen/Quint, Arnhem 1988 and material collected by the author

(9) Source: Report of an exchange visit by Kent Probation Service staff in Holland, 1991;. S Adelsberg

(10) *American Corrections* T. Clear and G. Cole: Brooks, Cole Publishing, California (2nd edition: 1990)

(11) *Ibid,* p 569

(12) *Partnership in Offender Supervision.* Mary Fielder. Greater Manchester Probation Service (1991)

(13) Report to Surrey Probation Committee, January 1991. I am indebted to Leon Spender, ACPO and Peter Spring, SPO, for much of the information in

this account.

(14) 'Doing Time in Deva', Thames Television: April 1991

(15) *Daily Mirror*, London, 10 April 1991.

Chapter 7 Developing Good Practice

Ian McNair

'Each scheme appeared to be built around creative, entrepreneurial individuals rather than carefully considered strategies, with the ever present risk that schemes could be at risk when the key individuals moved on'. (1)

This statement was in relation to the new Bail Information Scheme of the late 1980s. If the Audit Commission had existed in the 1970s, it would very likely have been making the same observations in respect of the new Community Service by Offenders Schemes. The parallells in development are fascinating and the differences intriguing. This chapter, as much as anything, reflects upon the development of good practice in community service and the ways in which it has come to be defined. It can be seen to have moved from a person centred, value based probation environment of the early 1970s, to the more mechanistic, process orientated, efficiency systems of the 1990s. Best practice is a synthesis of the two extremes. The development of community service has illustrated the tensions between these forces. The debate between service managers and practitioners, qualified and non-qualified staff and, uniquely to community service in the probation service, between service and beneficiary, have continued because offenders on community service orders have had varied experiences in widely variable schemes with very different staff groups. The movement from within community service that led to the establishment of National Standards can be seen as a response to the new managerialism of the 1980s. It grew from a desire for equity of practice between areas and schemes and a desire to understand and develop the *process* of community service. This chapter, however, deals with more than just process and National Standards. It looks also at the link between good practice and appropriate staffing and management; and the development of ACOP good practice guidelines following specially sponsored research.

For over one hundred years probation officers have carried responsibility for supervising offenders in the community. At its core, that relationship between officer and offender carried with it society's hopes of resolving criminal behaviour in a positive, humane and caring fashion. The advent of community service orders in 1973 gave the service a further opportunity, especially at that stage, to provide a real alternative to imprisonment for many thousands of offenders. It also provided a significant additional dimension to the officer/offender relationship in the form of the community. Probation staff, who had previously taken the offender into a 'casework' relationship, now went one stage further by consciously placing the offender into the community, thus taking on a direct responsibility for the public behaviour and attitudes of that offender. The community could see a clearer and more demonstrable link between the offender, the probation service and itself. The officer/offender interaction was no longer a 'private' matter conducted in an office or in the home. It became public. Staff of probation services now negotiated not with the 'proxy' public of the courts, but directly with the public itself.

From those early years came two themes to inform a continuing debate both within and, increasingly, outside of the service. This chapter focuses particularly on one of those themes which, although the language changes as time goes by, is represented now by National Standards, the codification of systems, the new managerialism and value for money. It is also important to consider the other theme, that of the role of the professional social worker in the probation service. The two themes are linked by concepts of accountability and by the tension that continues through the 1990s between public accountability and personal responsibility.

Before the 'system' thinking of the 1980s took hold, there was a deceptively low-key debate within the service around the composition of the staff team in community service. In 1979, Roger Williams (2) presented the seminal, and as yet unanswered, case for the critically important location of probation officers in community service. His theme was that the decisions to be made regarding the offender's progress onto, through and beyond a community service order, were as central to a probation officer's skills, training and experience as any other part of the service's operation. He made the telling observation that 'Assessment of work-party projects, for example, is not simply a case of *quantity* surveying in terms of tools, equipment and man-hours needed to complete them. There is also the question of what we might call *quality* surveying, that is, looking at the referral in terms of what the work would offer for the offender in terms of gaining self-respect and confidence in his abilities'. McIvor (3), to whom reference will be made later, provides us with a range of evidence to support how critical that aspect is to the outcome and impact of the community service order. As community service schemes developed, so different views were taken of the place of probation officers in community service. A study of community service orders by the University of Birmingham, commissioned in 1987 (4), looked at a range of schemes that varied from an extensive probation officer presence to no presence whatsoever.

It is helpful to reflect upon a more contemporary view from the 'Efficiency and Effectiveness Inspection of the Probation Service: The First Year', (5). A valuable exposition of the relative concepts of efficiency and effectiveness is applied to community service and the use of qualified probation officers. The definition proposed of *effectiveness* is related to success or otherwise in achieving intended results, while that for *efficiency* relates to the appropriate use of resources in achieving effectiveness and the avoidance of any unintended adverse consequences. The point is well made that efficiency and effectiveness 'need to be seen as relative concepts . . . public accountability requires that results should be measured wherever possible and that all the aspects of the service should be subject to regular systematic appraisal by management so that informed judgments can be made about outcomes'. The simple measurement of outcome, or of process, does not of itself enhance quality. It is the exercise of 'informed judgments' that guides the present and future direction of community service. Those judgments need to be informed not only by a strong sense of public accountability, but also by a strong sense of professional responsibility. Community service schemes, of necessity, must operate in a systematic way and the service at large has learnt much from community service about the process of administering community based orders. The service has learnt less about the broader management and professional judgments that have informed the operation of the best community service schemes. The report of HMI appears to struggle with this broader validity of the presence of probation staff when it says:

'The use of qualified probation officers for tasks normally undertaken by ancillary grades in community service was criticised in some areas. The committees concerned were asked to review the roles the probation officers played and the time they spent on duties not requiring professional qualified staff. The practice appeared to be based on *theoretical* grounds about the nature of the community service scheme that the area sought to provide. There would be little argument that some form of professional probation resource is required in community service to provide expertise in court work, the understanding of offenders behaviour and a contribution to the value base of the scheme. There was however little evidence for, and some argument against, the idea that probation officers acted more effectively and efficiently in the basic, day-to-day management of community service workers than well recruited and well trained ancillary staff.'

This bears further examination. The key aspect is in the appropriate definition, within community service, of the role of the probation officer and the role of specialist staff. Appropriateness also requires a clarity of management vision about the intended objectives of a community service scheme. If you define the objectives as the completion of 'x' number of hours in the shortest possible time, then that is a very different objective to ensuring that each offender on community service, and each beneficiary of the work completed, has a (mutually) beneficial experience of the community service order. One can begin to distinguish between at least two different sets of responsibilities. If the objectives of a community service scheme are weighted towards the latter example, then it may be appropriate to have probation officer staff ensuring the effectiveness of achieving that intended outcome. If the objective is simply the former, then the argument is not so strong. The former objectives are to do with process, the latter are to do with outcome. Issues of process are important, but it is the management of the offender through the process, rather than the process itself, that holds the true core of the probation task in community service. It is that focus which gives the probation service its 'unique selling point' in the market place and provides its key professional input to the community service order.

The basic day-to-day running of a community service scheme does not necessarily amount to a management exercise, but rather the routine administration of procedures within given guide-lines. The error of perception by some when looking at National Standards was that they were seen as prescribing the overall objectives or management of the scheme, when in fact they simply provided a framework within which the exercise of professional judgment is

105

enabled. One model is that probation officer staff manage the progress of offenders through the community service order, while other specialist staff administer the system through which those offenders progress. The 'staff-mix' in community service teams is a significant factor in the definition and achievement of best practice. It will influence the nature of a community service scheme and its objectives. The oft-heard debate between community service staff as to the relative value of the 'discipline breach' typifies the difference of view. The outcome of such debates influences key definitions around indicators of good practice and ultimately what constitutes a good scheme.

Definitions of good practice not only cover the process of the community service order, but also describe the management and practice role of staff within community service units. The ostensibly new and innovative 'quality' agenda can equally well be seen as the restatement of the best aspirations of professional practice of the best community service schemes. Similarly, the rediscovered 'partnership' agenda has always been common operational practice in good community service schemes. Early community service organisers will well remember the provision of the Powers of the Criminal Courts Act 1973, sched 3, para 10(3), which provided for payments to be made to 'any society or body in respect of their service' to the community service scheme. As further evidence that nothing is really new, the world of 'market-testing' may also have been anticipated by para 14(2) of the same Schedule, which allows for cross-area payments to probation committees to administer community service orders on offenders who reside in another area.

Thus the original legislation for community service orders provided an enabling base for the operation of community service schemes. Commentators from the 1970s and later (Pease *et al*) illustrate the range of developments as schemes were established nation wide. Regional groups of community service managers met together to support the development of schemes which readily established themselves as significant elements of local probation services. From the work of one of those regional groupings in the South West, came the material for a paper, presented to the National Community Service Conference at the University of Keele in March 1980, by Bruce Seymour (6). The paper's clear proposition is for implementation of standards of practice in community service. Seymour's contention that equity of service delivery is a proper aspiration and that community service lends itself to such a system because it is 'still a small enough field', provide an impetus to what was to become a national movement. Community service could not still be described as a 'small enough' field, but it remained a 'specific enough' field for it to become the first subject of National Standards in 1989.

In his presentation to the Keele Conference, Seymour distinguished between two categories of standard. By *general* standards he would mean 'principles like honesty, justice and integrity, as well as concepts like management'. By *specific* standards he would mean 'standards that apply to a specific situation or a specific type of activity'. The 'National Standards for Community Service', introduced in 1989, were a predictable mixture of both categories and that mix was reinforced by the absorption into, and consistency with, the composite 'National Standards for the Supervision of Offenders in the Community', introduced in 1992 (11). Accounts of those national community service conferences of the late 1970s and early 1980s are of more than historical interest. Within those accounts can be seen the range of concerns currently abroad within the service and which have provided much of the content for the debate 'whither community service?' in teams throughout the 1980s and 1990s. What is clear is that the hopes and ambitions of the 1970s and 1980s were the necessary prelude to the later introduction of National Standards and the recognition of the truly extensive impact of community service on sentencing patterns.

National Standards were initially promulgated in the Green Paper 'Punishment, Custody and the Community', published by the Home Office in July 1988. National Standards for community service orders were formally introduced in April 1989. They had a variable response from services, some of whom had community service schemes working at a level in excess of National Standards, while others appeared to struggle on some of the key indicators such as 'pick-up' time, or the period that elapsed between the Order being made at court and the offender starting work. In some quarters, the National Standards were seen as an irrelevance, and unnecessary external prescription, while in others they were welcomed. The concurrent publication in 1989 of the Audit Commission's Report on the Probation Service (1) underlined the need for, and value of, standards that sought to enhance consistency, demonstrate effectiveness, spread good practice, develop management systems and clarify lines of accountability.

The Home Office, in consultation with the Association of Chief Officers of Probation (ACOP) and others, reviewed the impact of the National Standards and concluded that the key findings were:

'That the number and rate of community service breaches had increased; the proportion of community service orders revoked had remained stable despite that increased breach rate; breach was occurring after fewer unacceptable absences; 'pick-up' times had remained fairly stable, with a slight increase in long delays'.

The review methodology was not seen to be particularly effective however and, therefore, this evaluation of the impact of National Standards was not particularly influential.

ACOP then commissioned its own review of National Standards. This was carried out by Christine Wilkinson and Neil Thomas of the University of Birmingham (8) and led to an Action Plan being published by the Association for the guidance of service managers. The view was taken that monitoring required by the Home Office at that time did not lend itself to the gathering of data in a way which could lead to an informed analysis. Accordingly, a research project was designed whereby staff from a selection of varied areas (9) were systematically questioned about the implementation of the Standards. The review subsequently reported on the aspects of the implementation of National Standards, the impact on resources, on sentencing, on practice and on changes in management practice.

With regard to the impact on resources, an aspect ignored by Home Office monitoring, it was found that in three of the nine areas, no extra money had been budgeted, mainly on the premise that the budget was already adequate and high standards had already been achieved. Of the areas requiring extra resources, the major requirement was for more sessional supervisors to manage the increased groupwork sessions. National Standards had prescribed arrangements for the placement of offenders into work groups on the premise that this reinforced the discipline and punitive aspects of community service. There is a widely and properly held view within the service that equal discipline and effort is required of offenders on individual placements. The focus on the work group rather than the individual placement reinforces the view that National Standards emphasise process rather than outcome. Most areas which sought extra resources expected an increase in the number of orders, but this was, initially at least, not borne out in practice. The money seemed to have been used in closer supervision of the same (overall) number of offenders and additional time and reports needed for the larger number of breach cases.

The impact on sentencing was a proper focus for the University of Birmingham's review, especially as one aim in introducing National Standards was to 'generate greater confidence in community service with sentencers'. The profile of community service was certainly raised with courts as a consequence of the implementation of National Standards, and it can safely be concluded that sentencers knew more about the administration and management of community service schemes. However, the research indicated that it was extremely difficult to conclude that this had an impact on sentencing. Four of the areas examined showed a decrease in the number of community service orders following the arrival of National Standards and five reported increases. The research showed a considerable lack of uniformity between probation areas and principally there were very different policy level interpretations of some standards. Considerable scope had been left for discretion and a lack of resources had caused some pragmatic decisions to be taken on adherence to some standards. The conclusion, therefore, was that the application of standards did appear to have increased the confidence of courts, but had not affected, at that stage, and in general terms, sentencing practice. Taking what is now a longer term view, there has been a significant rise in the number of community service orders which, by 1991 had reached 42,500 new orders in the year, representing 13% of Crown Court sentences and 7% of magistrates' courts sentences.

Other aspects of National Standards seemed to have a negative effect on practice. For example, groupwork designed to improve the appearance of amenities in a neighbourhood, including litter collection and clearance, could be seen as bordering on degrading and boring for the offender. This made for difficulties between supervisor and offender. Within community service there is a widely held view that work which is demanding, personally fulfilling and which can also improve the appearance of the neighbourhood *can* still be found. Paradoxically, due to the growth in breach cases, the time spent on their preparation and prosecution had resulted in staff being less available to research out or create those kinds of community service work. Research carried out by McIvor (3) should cause us to be concerned that priority was given here to process, impeding the equal priority of the quality of work experience, a critical determinant of outcome. The Survey of Community Service Standards in Northern Ireland (9) would also reinforce the significant nature of the community service task for the offender. The review work gave little insight into the arrangements for work for black offenders or for women offenders. The Probation Inspectorate did subsequently begin to address some of the gender issues in its report on Women Offenders and Probation Service Provision (10). Research is currently in progress around a series of gender issues in community service. It is clear that anti-discriminatory practice is good practice. The provision of child care arrangements, sensible working hours and appropriate community service tasks is applicable across the board. It has been, and probably remains a fact, that many women offenders were deemed by pobation officers not to be 'suitable' by virtue of child care responsibilities for community service orders only to be sentenced to imprisonment. There are, equally, a wide range of issues centred around black offenders and community service schemes, variable recommendation rates, inappropriate placement arrangements and poor levels of care in communication. *Chapter 5* of this book focuses particularly on those issues concerned with women offenders. It is a management responsibility to ensure policies are in place and monitored for efficiency. The final area of practice impact described by the ACOP review was around the enforcement of orders where, again, we get a further insight into a different perception of community service from probation officers and specialist community service staff. The research indicated that there were differences between the two groups of staff in their expectations following breach. Community service officers mostly expected severe penalties and probation officers tended to look for a 'disciplinary' fine. The review indicated important problems in a strict (literal) use of standards in accepting reasons for adherence; in collating reliable evidence to support an opinion, or a decision, leading to breach action; and whether the system should be largely mechanistic or open to some degree of negotiation. Later versions of the National Standards have helped to clarify some of these issues.

The final focus of the ACOP review was on changes in management practice. The most important point seemed to be that whatever kind of organisation structure there is for the management of community service, the research does not show any signficant differences in outcome. Outcome was defined as those measures of efficiency addressed by the National Standards. There remain opportunities for future research on the organisational variations and upon staff roles within community service schemes. The review did feel able to conclude that probation services with a centralised structure for community service did appear to have less inconsistency within their area than those with a decentralised community service scheme. The review also showed the need for clear management guidelines in relation to community service practice even though National Standards were in place. Interestingly, the review evidenced this by demonstrating that the staff member who holds responsibility for breach action appears to be a crucial determinant in relation to the outcome of that particular case. Good management practice also encompasses vital health and safety issues, the particular problems of offenders in rural areas and effective management information systems.

Having considered the findings of Wilkinson and Thomas' ACOP sponsored review of the implementation of National Standards, the Association then produced an Action Plan covering the areas detailed in that review work. One of the most detailed of those Action Plans was that to do with the effect on practice. Reflecting the theme of this chapter, it was felt important to restate the aims of community service and then to define more closely the tasks that required to be undertaken to achieve those aims. Further, those tasks were to reflect a clear focus for each scheme, which in turn would lead on to a discrete set of outcomes.

The aims identified for community service by ACOP reflected the twin areas of accountability for any community service scheme. The first aim was to 'ensure the highest possible rate of completion, by fair and equitable practice, consistent with National Standards and local policy'. It is obviously a clear starting point that a high rate of completion is a necessary outcome, even if only on the simple grounds of cost effectiveness. This is particularly important, bearing in mind the higher breach rate which occurred with the advent of National Standards, for these resulted not only in extra resources being dedicated to enforcement work, but also led to a significant number of offenders being sentenced to imprisonment. Fair and equitable practice was an important consideration and needed to be reinforced by local policy within the framework of National Standards. The second aim was to ensure 'that community service work is of maximum benefit to the community'. At a simple level this aim means just what it says; but it also acknowledges that the community is best served by successful community service schemes, which provide offenders with a significant and purposeful experience under a community service order, the nature of which will influence their attitudes towards re-offending.

In pursuance of those aims, five key tasks were defined. The first was to ensure that there were clear workload management systems and job specifications in place to enable community service staff to perform their roles efficiently. The importance of these cannot be over stated. Similarly, the deployment of staff in community service should seek to maximise both the rate of successful completions and the value of the experience to the offender. The third task relates to process. Clear procedural guidelines for the review and, where appropriate, the breach of, the offender subject to a community service order, should be in place. The enforcement of the community service order begins from the moment it is imposed and requirements for clear procedures for record keeping and review of the order are a necessary pre-requisite to good practice. Those procedures should be informed by explicit arrangements to ensure that effective equal opportunity exists for offenders, in respect of selection for, and completion of, community service orders. This, the fourth task, has become a more discrete aspect of community service operations and especially reflects the probation service's appreciation of the differential impact of systems of justice and systems of administration on different parts of the community. The final task was that there should be a clear recognition that the concerns and expectations of the beneficiaries should be a key consideration in arranging and progressing work placements. It is in achieving a proper balance between the needs of the offender and the needs of the community that community service schemes can best demonstrate good practice.

The ACOP Action Plan went on to describe three focal points that need to be borne in mind throughout community service work. These were that clear procedures should be in place to ensure that proper regard is paid to issues of

Health and Safety, insurance, and risk assessment. The last is of particular significance, when offenders who, in many cases, would otherwise have been serving custodial sentences, are consciously placed in environments where, amongst the beneficiaries, will be potential vulnerable members of the public. The second focus would be that the range of beneficiaries should reflect the community served by the community service scheme. This is an important equal opportunities aspiration and in many probation areas we now see the development of work opportunities under community service schemes which are particularly focused upon the victim. Whilst community service directed towards individual victims is, as yet, in a very early stage of development, the focus of work on victimised communities is becoming a more common phenomena within schemes. Examples abound across the country and are illustrated in other chapters of this book, for example, vandalised property being repaired, of crime prevention and security measures being provided by community service schemes, and more generally, the community being enriched by the contribution of offenders or groups of offenders where previously those offenders had despoiled the area. The third focus was thus, that community service schemes should provide tangible opportunities for offenders to contribute to crime prevention. Again many schemes can provide examples of situations where offenders on community service have enhanced crime prevention measures or demonstrably improved the physical aspects of a community and then subsequently developed a proprietorial attitude towards that work.

Outcomes, other than simple completion rates, are more difficult. Quality of experience for the offender and the quality of service received by the beneficiary are significant measures. Very few probation services at this stage have systems in place to measure that quality of experience or quality of service. The Citizen's Charter agenda and issues of quality service which are by definition focused upon the user, or beneficiary, of services, have served to highlight this aspect of community service schemes. The final outcome proposed by the ACOP Action Plan was that the reduction of fear of crime is a proper objective and that this can be demonstrated through the positive alteration of stereotypes of the offender and of the victim through the community service experience. Again, very many schemes will provide tangible and comprehensive examples of individual people, groups or communities, expressing a marked change of perception of offenders as a consequence of community service work. That can be particularly and profoundly the case where offenders working under community service orders, can work either in their own community or in the community against which they have specifically offended.

In the survey of community service standards from Northern Ireland (9), a group of beneficiaries were questioned about their experience of community service. The vast majority of those beneficiaries were not only satisfied with the standard of work done by the offenders, but most regarded the offenders on community service orders as 'conscientious, punctual, enthusiastic and self disciplined'. Interestingly a majority of them did conclude that they thought the work had been of benefit to the offender as well as to themselves. This research also would support the proposition that in a good community service scheme one clear aspect of achievement is that work tasks are completed, or demonstrable progress is constantly apparent. This aspect is important, both for the beneficiary and for the offender. In the Northern Ireland survey, 50% of tasks were completed within three weeks and the vast majority were completed within ten weeks.

Best practice also focuses on opportunities which maximise contact between offenders and beneficiaries of the service. In looking at the question of variable contact between offender and beneficiary, Lount says (9):

'These considerations have implications for the matching of offender to task, not just in terms of the offender's ability and skill to do a job, but also to take into account the opportunity for a personal relationship with the recipient of the service. It is feasible that some offenders need the meaningful contact more than others; the reciprocal relationship would provide the offender with a sense of value, of dignity and the opportunity to give, thus possibly helping to neutralise the damage of self image consequent on involvement with crime and the subsequent criminal stigma'.

This emphasis is one that finds reinforcement with the Social Work in Scotland Group (15) which also recommended that schemes actively involve offenders in the allocation to work placements:

'The involvement of the offender in the matching process did not have an effect on completion or compliance, but did appear to result in a slightly more satisfactory match being achieved as evidenced by the offenders' attitude towards the work they carried out. The interviewing of offenders after an order has been made, in the attempt to engage them actively in this decision making process, has associated cost implications and may not have a substantial impact on the responses to community services. It may however, in some instances, prevent subsequent placement breakdown and may increase the likelihood of the work being of value to the offender, which is in itself an objective of the Social Work in Scotland group guidelines and was one of the originally intended purposes of community service'.

This further refinement, ie the involvement of the offender in the matching process, may well be one which is increasingly found in good quality community service schemes.

National Standards define good practice in the range of processes within the order. They also include a focus on some aspects of practice that occur *before* an order is made and principally those of equal opportunities, proper consideration of the management of risk, and targeting. The early phase of the community service order is considered to be particularly significant in the successful completion of that order. There is as yet little formal research to substantiate some of the assertions made in National Standards, although many make good sense and reflect considered professional experience. It is good practice to start offenders working promptly under community service orders, but that should not be at the expense of short cuts on risk assessment or proper and due consideration of appropriate placement opportunities. It is better that an offender be properly introduced to a placement and properly instructed in such issues as health and safety at work rather than there being a sense of unnecessary haste. Similarly, whilst it is desirable that the order proceeds at an active pace and we have seen earlier that the offender does need to have a sense of progress, undue haste can be counter-productive and can certainly detract from the quality of the experience. There is no research which demonstrates that orders completed quickly are more effective in terms of future re-conviction rates. Indeed, there would be some experience that a steady pace of completion over some months, enabling the offender to establish significant relationships with the beneficiaries, or the benefiting community, are of more benefit. An important aspect at the start of a new community service order is the clarity of contract between the parties involved. National Standards require supervision plans and these are as applicable to the community service experience as they are to any other form of community supervision. They are particularly necessary in the context of the combination order. It is important that the offender recognises and owns the content of the contract specified for community service and is encouraged to develop a strong sense of personal responsibility for the successful completion. The principle of informed consent is mentioned in National Standards and this needs to be truly the case to ensure the best possible response.

Good practice, early in the order, also includes the best possible matching of individual abilities and skills to tasks; improving motivation and demonstrating to the offender that he or she can learn from the experience, too.

A characteristic of a good community service scheme is also the presence of an ongoing, consistent and comprehensive review of the offender's progress through the order. This is reinforced by those schemes able to follow up absences in person and who have comprehensive systems for the analysis of the reasons for absence from work. The determination of whether an absence is acceptable, or unacceptable, is crucial in the process of enforcement of the community service order and is the point at which the best professional judgments need to be made.

At this point it is helpful to consider the broad context of 'quality', as applied to the community service operation. Perhaps the key focus of any quality system is that the 'user's view' is paramount. Within community service there could be said to be three users for whom the issue of quality is significant, albeit for different reasons. The view from the court, as a user of the probation service, will significantly determine the number of community service orders made and what action will be taken on those orders returned to court for breach. The view of the beneficiary, as a user of the service provided by the community service scheme, will be paramount in the quality of that work, the availability of work in the future, and the potential for a change in perception of that beneficiary and their community of the offender. The third aspect is that of the offender, as a user of the community service order opportunity, administered and managed by the probation service. All three elements should be considered by probation services when assessing the quality of their community service schemes. Simple techniques to capture user feedback, such as questionnaires, sampling, research projects, user panels and termination interviews should feature as a matter of good practice. Much of the relationship with users can be proactively managed and indeed the requirement to produce annual reports and information leaflets is but one aspect of that. Discontent from those three user groups will show itself in different ways.

The courts will not make so many community service orders if they are not satisfied; beneficiaries and benefiting communities will be less likely to agree to provide work opportunities for offenders on community service orders and finally, the offenders themselves will perform less well and be less positively influenced by the experience if it is of poor quality. Over the years courts have come to regard community service orders most favourably and they continue to be properly impressed by demonstrable performance indicators primarily to do with process. The dearth of longitudinal studies on re-conviction rates still means that many of the desirable outcomes perceived of community service remain a matter of aspiration or of limited statistical significance.

It is when one examines the relevance of the Citizen's Charter, the consumer's perspective, and concepts of user choice to the offender element of this tripartite relationship to the probation service and its community service schemes, that some of the more interesting aspects arise.

In 1990 the Home Office issued the Victim's Charter (13). Only two statements in that document were specific to probation. One related to the preparation of release plans for life-sentence prisoners having due regard to the victim, or the victim's family, wishes and interests. The other should begin to bear specifically upon the work of community service schemes in that it asks the question, 'How far does the Service work with the victims and their representative groups? What consideration is given to victims' interests in aspects of the Probation Services work?'

There are scattered throughout the country a few innovative projects around issues of reparation and mediation to the victims. Many of them have different approaches and provide a different rationale for their involvement in reparation and mediation. Victim offender mediation is one type of scheme. Such schemes are at a very early stage of development, although their proponents would keenly attest to the actual and potential benefit of their endeavour. There is a continuum which could include an offender under a community service order making reparation to the specific victim or victims of their offending behaviour. Such a progression is a difficult one. It demands great skill and perception on the part of those involved, and for some victims would be seen as undesirable. The victim's right to privacy and to no further intrusion into their life is vitally important. Notwithstanding that, there must be considerable potential for the appropriate reparation by offenders to their victims through the medium of a community service order. That is a broad principle of community service which can be traced back to the Wootton Report. There are more victims of offences against property and particularly against domestic property, than there are, say, of assault against the person. The former category lends itself more readily to reparation than the latter, where different forms and expressions may be desirable.

It is clear that courts, at all levels throughout the two decades of the existence of community service orders, have recognised the principal of reparation to the community by offenders and that rationale will often have been included in the sentencing process. It will also have featured in many pre-sentence reports to courts in proposing a sentence of community service. Latterly, a fresh area for the exploration of this potential has shown itself through the combination order.

Again, at its best, the practice relating to combination orders proposes a theoretical line of work with the offender, which, having arranged an appropriate and relevant work placement under community service can, through the probation order aspect of the combination order, provide room for real reflection upon the value of that work both to the beneficiary and also, with real potential, to the offender. There are offenders, many of whom find themselves on probation orders now or on combination orders in the future, who do not relate positively either to the community at large or to individuals specifically. There is a potential for community service to address that difficulty. As McIvor writes (7):

'The broad nature of the work performed or the setting in which it is carried out will appear to be less important than the characteristics of placements themselves. To maximise the value of CS for the offenders, schemes should endeavour to provide placements which maximise the potential contact between the offender and the beneficiaries which can offer the opportunity for the acquisition of new skills and which require offenders to undertake work which they will perceive as being of considerable benefit to the recipients of the services'.

McIvor goes on in another article concerned with quality (16):

'The most interesting results emerged . . . when re-conviction was examined in relation to offenders' experience on CS. Offenders who found CS to be particularly worthwhile were slightly less likely than others to be re-convicted, they were re-convicted less often in the three years following sentence and they were markedly less likely to be re-convicted of offences involving dishonesty, such as burglary and theft'.

She went on:

'The quality of placement experience was most influential among offenders who were unemployed when sentenced or who had, as a result of their offending, previously been subject to some form of statutory supervision as an adult or as a child. Personal development and experience of being valued are likely to be particularly significant for offenders who are lacking in confidence at the outset and who perhaps had little or no opportunity to contribute positively to their local communities in the past'.

From the offenders' perspective, (which has most commonly been the focus of probation work) there is now considerable research evidence to support the principle that amongst many elements of good practice in community service schemes, one in particular must focus upon the assessment of offenders prior to placement in work, the nature and characteristics of that work, and especially the potential for interaction between the offender performing the community service work and the beneficiary for whom that work is being performed. The work of Lount (9) in looking at the experience of National Standards in Northern Ireland, does point up some key elements of good practice to enhance beneficiaries' levels of satisfaction with community service. They do need to feel that

115

community service staff are in touch with them and their needs and that these are reviewed regularly. Individual offenders or work parties should never be placed with beneficiaries without there having been previously a clear explanation of the process of the community service work, assurances given about responsible supervision of offenders, and also the beneficiaries' right to, and process of, complaining or seeking redress should the experience prove not to be a positive one for them. The dialogue that needs to exist between, in particular, community service officers, but also significantly with community service supervisors of work groups and voluntary agencies supervisors, must inform the probation officer's key task of assessment and placement of offenders on community service. Those interactions should lead to the establishment of levels of quality service to beneficiaries which are beyond the level of merely sufficient. The whole quality agenda itself is an opportunity to restate the best of professional practice and the best of management achievements.

Community service is one of the most consumer orientated areas of probation service activities. Courts and beneficiaries see that very clearly. Reinforced by the Criminal Justice Act 1991, concepts of restrictions on liberty mean that the offender experiences the community service order in a more immediate and focussed manner than many of the other programmes open to the probation service.

The search for best practice in community service should not, as some of the arguments in this chapter illustrate, be restricted to those aspects which are currently measurable and visible. It is a contemporary seduction of the 1990s that quality principally relates to measurable and visible aspects of practice.

There can be an aridity and superficiality to community service National Standards if taken literally. Those aspects of community service national standards that are measured may very well be to do with pace of work, frequency of attendance and number of unacceptable absences. National Standards are only there as a framework for the expectation and requirements for supervision. They are there to enable professional judgment to be exercised within a framework of accountability, by encouraging imagination, initiative and innovation in the development of good practice and by ensuring that supervision is delivered fairly, consistently and without discrimination.

The initial reaction to the first version of National Standards in community service was to diminish their positive contribution and rather to see them instead as an administrative and bureaucratic imposition upon schemes. As ever though, community service staff rose to the challenge and once they saw beyond the language to the support that National Standards gave to best practice, so their experience has been positive. One particularly helpful contribution from National Standards for the supervision of community service orders has been that section to do with the management of risk. The Standards anticipate that more serious offenders than before may receive a community sentence as a consequence of the Criminal Justice Act 1991. While the probation service cannot guarantee the conduct of any offender given a community sentence, the management of risk, both of serious re-offending and of serious harm to the public, where relevant, is an important part of the work of the service and the tensions it has to manage. National Standards proposed ways in which risk can be managed effectively and saw those as including:

'Producing local practice guidelines on working with high risk offenders, including advice on the safety and protection of staff; adopting strategies for the conduct of CSOs designed to reduce risk to the public and . . . ensuring that probation staff are vigilant for indications of possible risk of serious harm to the public from offenders, and make clear such concerns, where relevant to courts (eg through PSRs or breach action) and to line management'.

Community service staff have always been very aware of the element of risk to the community through their placement of offenders on community service work. When schemes are routinely placing offenders in, for example, old people's homes, voluntary organisations and other agencies, assessment of risk is an immediate and relevant one relating to the public world and to public accountability. As such it does at times have a different strength to it than views expressed and decisions made in the more private world of the probation order. As individual probation staff have moved into and eventually out of community service schemes into other operational areas of the probation service, so they have taken that experience with them. Amongst the key elements of that has been a closer appreciation of risk management.

Those creative, entrepreneurs of the early community service schemes in the 1970s were both a product and exemplification of their time. The skills and qualities they exhibited were necessary for the secure foundation of the new scheme. The success of this most significant community based sentence owes much to them. Similarly, the effect that community service staff, of all grades, have had within the probation service, within the criminal justice system and within local communities, has been profound. Whilst the very proper concerns of the 1980s were to codify and standardise community service by offenders, so now a 'new professionalism' begins to move centre stage. Debates about operational practice need to reflect the value-added dimension as much as the value for money dimension. It may be financially cheaper to use work groups in community service but it may not be more effective if we properly understand our experience and research. The contact the offender has with the beneficiary appears to have a key significance for best practice. The promise of community service schemes linking with voluntary organisations (facilitated by sched 3 to the Powers of the Criminal Courts Act 1973) has only intermittently been fulfilled. The re-awakened partnership agenda may open up that potential again, not only for the provision of individual and group placements, but also to emphasise the core activity of service by offenders to the community. Probation services have demonstrated a great capacity for innovation and change over the years and community service is one of the key areas of evidence. From the springboard of National Standards, the challenge for probation services and their community service schemes lies not only in efficient procedures, but more critically in effective outcomes.

Twenty years experience of community service by offenders has enabled the probation service to develop much *excellent* practice in the field. It is that excellence of practice, as much as economy, efficiency and effectiveness, which should inform community service schemes in the future.

REFERENCES

(1) *The Probation Service: Promoting Value for Money,* Audit Commission, 1989

(2) *Probation Officer Skills in Community Service,* Roger Williams in Probation Journal, vol 26, March 1979

(3) *Community Service in Scotland: A Summary of Findings and Conclusions,* Gill McIvor, Social Work Research Centre, University of Stirling, September 1989

(4) *Study of Community Service Orders:* Unpublished Report, Department of Social Policy & Social Work University of Birmingham (Commissioned in 1987)

(5) *Efficiency & Effectiveness, Inspection of the Probation Service: The First Year,* Home Office (HMI), October 1990

(6) Unpublished Paper by Bruce Seymour, RSDO (South West), delivered to National Community Service Conference University of Keel, March 1980

(7) *Community Service Work Placements,*Gill McIvor in Howard Journal, vol 30 no 1, February 1991

(8) *Community Service Orders: Monitoring National Standards,* Association of Chief Officers of Probation, July 1991

(9) *Community Service Standards for Northern Ireland,* M Lount, University of Ulster, April 1991

(10) *Report on Women Offenders and Probation Service Provision,* Home Office (HMI), July 1991

(11) *National Standards for the Supervision of Offenders in the Community,* Home Office, August 1992

(12) *Going Straight: Developing Good Practice in the Probation Service,* Audit Commission: Occasional Paper No 16, October 1991

(13) *Victims' Charter: A Statement of the Rights of Victims of Crime,* Home Office, 1990

(14) *Assessing Competence: Scientific Process or Subjective Inference? Do we really see 'it'?,* Hazel Kemshall in Social Work Education, vol 12, no 1, April

(15) *National Standards and Objectives for the Operation of CS by Offenders Schemes in Scotland*, Scottish Office Social Work Services Group, 1989, Edinburgh

(16) *Quality Counts*, Gill McIvor in Probation Journal, vol 39, no 3, September 1992

Chapter 8 A Week in the Life Of . . .

Joe Woods

No book on community service could be complete without a view of the 'sharp end'. Policy and practice guidelines may provide an essential framework but the reality of community service lies in the Sunday morning struggle to get up and join the work group on time; in the uneasy tensions of a group testing out a new supervisor; in the nervousness of a single community service worker starting a new placement and in the sudden flare-up which demands immediate intervention and which may yet end in court with breach proceedings.

A working day may see all these, yet miss the patient negotiations for a new work project with a community group, still uncertain about the effect of a group of offenders among them; or the exhilaration of a well completed piece of work and the gratitude of the beneficiary. A caseload of 50 or so orders provides a community service officer with a rich and diverse mix of offenders, opportunities and problems. To try and capture these we asked Joe Woods to record, diary like, a week in the life of a community service organiser. Other names, of course, have been changed in the interests of both the innocent and the guilty.

• • • • •

Monday

It's 9.00 am on Monday morning as Brian Bellingham arrives at the community service office. The phone rings and he takes the call from the organiser of the local Age Concern Office. Minnie Brown the 83 year old woman who had a team of workers over the weekend to paint and decorate in her bungalow had rung Age Concern as she was a bit upset at a paint drip on her window. It was not Brian's weekend covering community service and George Dunn who was community service assistant on duty was out re-fuelling the vans after the mileage of that weekend.

'Well thanks for the call. Look, we have our team review meeting this morning so I will bring it up there and we will get back to you. Someone will visit Minnie as soon as possible I'm sure.'

Brian put the phone down and turned to one of his colleagues, Jean Webster—'Well that's a good start to the week—9.00 am and I have already had the first complaint. I wonder if George knows anything about this?'

Dowerin is a large town on the edge of some beautiful National Park moorland in the heart of the Midlands. With a population of over 100,000 people and covering a densely populated urban area, as well as a large rural area, the community service office is a busy place. The office supervised between 120 and 150 orders per month before the Criminal Justice Act 1991 was implemented in October 1992. However, nine months later the orders seem to have stabilised at around the 200 mark and the team has been strengthened by an additional post of a community service officer to help to cope with the workload.

The Unit is run by a full time probation officer, four community service officers, one full time secretary and a workshop manager. The CS office is in the same complex as the probation office and probation centre which was converted from a disused fire station and includes a day centre and a wood workshop. Recently, because of a lack of space, the community service office and tool store has been moved into vacant garage premises next door to the probation centre and this includes space to park the three mini buses and trailers. The move was viewed with mixed feelings by the CS team because of the fear that community service would become even more isolated and marginalised from the main body of probation work. However, the community service team were also looking forward to having their own office space and sufficient room to organise a proper tool store with health and safety equipment and secure garaging for the previously often vandalised minibuses. The community service team had hitherto always shared office accommodation with field staff and John Sleeman, the senior probation officer responsible for all community service in the county of Midshire was concerned that the feelings which did exist of 'us and them' would be exacerbated by the move. It never ceased to amaze John that after 20 years of community service orders being organised by the probation service an attitude still prevailed that offenders on community service orders changed and became different people to those clients being supervised on probation orders. John believed strongly that the skills of probation officers working with offenders were vital not just to probation supervision but also to community service. The initial assessment by the probation officer was crucial in affecting the final outcome of success or failure when an offender was placed on community service. The need for field probation officers to confer with community service on potentially difficult offenders was also vital at that stage so that the community service team could organise suitable placements or supervisors and work parties to take into account the difficulties of that individual.

During their monthly meeting, John and Gina Lawrence, the probation officer running the community service unit, spent a proportion of the session deciding on a planned strategy to try and ensure that the community service team did not become separated from the probation field team. They decided that Gina would produce a discussion document for report writers and field probation officers to look at concerning the offenders who should be referred to the community service team. The county operates a policy that all offenders are suitable for community service but that those with histories of violence to authority figures, and sex offenders, must be discussed before a recommendation is made to court so that the safety of both staff and the general public can be considered. Others who need to be referred were those with particular difficulties which would need pre-planning to accommodate them on the scheme—individuals with child care or other dependent relatives to look after and no resources of their own; people who are receiving invalidity pension or long term sickness benefit, who have to get clearance from the local DHSS adjudicating officer so that benefit is unaffected. Lastly, those people with chronic drink or drug problems which would undoubtedly affect their attendance at community service. This document would form the basis of a discussion between Gina and each field team where she would discuss the issues with her colleagues as an agenda item at their team meeting. At least it was a start to a plan to try and ensure some positive communication between two areas of probation work essentially involving the same people!

The team

But back to Monday morning and the weekly team meeting around which the whole scheme revolved. Gina now looked forward to the planning meetings; her enthusiasm about community service had been well received by some of her team, although other members had tried to ensure that any changes did not take place. The first six months had not been easy as she tried to grapple with a completely different job from anything she had experienced as a field probation officer. However she had strongly held views that each offender must be given equal access to work parties and placements; that some individuals needed more positive input and help to get through their order than others; that the community service unit was there to basically assist individuals to complete their order; that working on the order should be a positive and rewarding learning experience; and that her social work skills would be invaluable to help those struggling to complete their order by assisting them to overcome some of their basic problems. These views were, however, not in accord with George's belief that community service was essentially a punishment, based on physical labour. Anything an individual achieved from the order was an admitted bonus, but work groups were, he thought, primarily there to help the community; in particular disadvantaged disabled people and the elderly.

George was a painter and decorator by trade who had worked for the local borough council until taking early retirement. He had been a supervisor initially and had now been a community service officer for over ten years.

Jane's main interest lay in the environmental projects; as a volunteer worker for the British Conservation Volunteers, Jane pushed strongly for wider tasks which would benefit the whole community and did involve physical labour such as footpath clearances, hedge laying, dry stone walling, tree planting and other 'green' projects.

However Gina drew support from both Brian Bellingham and Mike Bennett who made up the rest of the community service officers. Mike had left his trade as a garage mechanic to work as a care assistant in a residential home for young people run by social services. As a black worker he had developed a great interest in working with disadvantaged youngsters who had offended and this led him towards voluntary work with the probation service and then a full-time community service assistant post. Mike's interest was in developing work projects for individuals and groups from the ethnic minority sections in Dowerin. The south of the town had an established Afro Caribbean population and to a lesser extent a growing Muslim population—swelled by the settlement of a number of refugee families from the Afghanistan/Iran border area. Brian had made a decision in his mid-30's to change career from an engineer for a large local manufacturing industry. He took redundancy, started studying sociology at night school, working for the local volunteer bureau and also doing some relief work for the local probation hostel on night shifts. The most recent recruit to the team, because of the large increase in orders since the implementation of the Criminal Justice Act 1991, Brian had taken over the development of individual placements in the community. He firmly believed in the worth of these placements to give offenders a sense of responsibility and trust, as well as offering a completely new experience and often one which provided good learning opportunities and some potential for the future.

Gina had worked hard with the team to develop some uniformity of approach and the need for teamwork, sharing ideas and communicating with each other. Sometimes this had seemed an uphill task—but after 12 months Gina could see some progress towards developing good quality consistent practice which, wherever possible, took into account the needs of the individual within the boundaries of National Standards. The agenda for the team meeting included the regular weekly items of reviewing last weeks work; planning the next week; reviewing current placements and potential individuals for placement; ensuring that the 'sin' sheets (failure to attend lists) had been followed up and any other business items. The team this week were also to discuss how they were going to introduce the recently produced good practice guidelines for community service placements. A further item was the co-ordination of interviews of three potential sessional supervisors on Thursday; and the new magistrates visiting the scheme on Saturday.

Even before the meeting started, Gina learnt that a young woman, Karen Macinlay, had been to see the duty officer at the probation office to say she had been put on an 80 hour order at a court outside the area on Friday afternoon and she wanted to know who to see as she had been told to report at 10.00 am today.

'Oh, that will be the call I got on Friday', Jane said. 'I have put it in the diary as an appointment for today for an initial interview. The referring court officer from Piltshire said the community service order was made even though a probation order was recommended as Karen has a number of difficulties besides her offending. I know some of the background so I will interview her'.

The team meeting
After arranging to make a call to the Age Concern work project which had led to the early telephone call, the next period of the meeting was spent reviewing the progress of the work party projects —three or four work parties each day, and an evening work group on Tuesday. Most of the projects last week had been proceeding with no apparent difficulty and with the summer in full swing there were numerous individual garden projects to fill in the gaps between the regular weekly on-going and longer term projects.

There had been three incidents during the week which Gina wanted to discuss with the team besides the paint drip. The first occurred when one of the community service workers refused to work because he had no suitable work clothes. The man, Arthur Warslow, who had a history of mental instability and violence towards authority figures, had told Brian that the police had taken his clothes for forensic testing and he could not work. Brian offered him overalls and boots but Arthur then became abusive and threatened to knock Brian's head off and break Gina's legs with a baseball bat. Arthur had then stormed out of the office and not been seen since. Gina told the team that after discussion with the senior probation officer and assistant chief probation officer, Arthur was suspended from the scheme and the senior probation officer would write to him telling him that he was to be taken back to court for breach proceedings because he had refused to follow work directions and that his behaviour was unreasonable.

The second incident involved a recently appointed supervisor who the team felt had been 'conned' by his team—the team had cleared bracken and brush wood from a wildlife reserve for the local bird watchers association and had then started a bonfire to get rid of the debris. Simon Keller, the supervisor, had left his jumper on the path. After collecting more brush with three of the party, Simon came back to find his jumper gone and the two lads tending the fire disclaiming any knowledge of it but saying a group of young people had passed by and probably nicked it. After some discussion David could not get any further information but believed the lads burnt his jumper. Gina told the team that as David is unemployed and short of money, it has been agreed that the service will replace his jumper, out of the tools and equipment budget!

Lastly the warden of the Earlswood Residential Community Home for the elderly had written to the team extolling the virtues of the team's latest development, a luncheon club and activities afternoon for the elderly residents of this warden controlled flat complex.

The warden had written in especially to thank Brian and Mike who had organised the lunch club and the subsequent trips; first to the local indoor bowls club and second to the Meadowbank Shopping Centre. The supervisor, Sarah Bond, had been praised for her abilities to get the best out of her work group and show them how to prepare and serve the meal and then take a small group on their outing. The warden appreciated the hard work involved and wanted to pass on the thanks of the residents who had benefited so far.

The work projects for the next week were planned, supervisors allocated and a new project introduced which would take up a reasonable amount of time over a long period. This was a project for a town centre junior school to develop an area of disused overgrown land adjacent to their tennis courts and to make an allotment area and 'smell and feel' garden to be used by disabled and blind children from the nearby assessment nursery. This project also involved building a fish pond, fencing the area and laying paths and it would be open for the local community to use as visitors. The schools Parent Teachers Association had raised the money with the help of a European Urban Development Grant; community service were providing the free labour force and would work at times alongside both the school children and their volunteer parents.

After reviewing the 'sin' sheets, it was agreed that three individuals were to be breached as they now had three unacceptable absences; a further person was suspended from working having failed to attend and not offered any excuse at all, after breach proceedings had been taken out last week; two more offenders were offered appointments to see Gina to discuss their progress after two unacceptable absences and a number of individuals were to be asked for proof of last weeks absences. One was to be transferred to another area.

At this point Jane interjected that 'It's probably appropriate to bring in my interview with Karen Macinlay. I think this could be a very interesting order—with the emphasis on interesting. It seems that Karen has three young children all under the age of five and Karen is just 21 years old. She is a single parent, has no experience of paid or voluntary work and has had a number of periods of hospitalisation for acute depression, linked to suicide attempts. Also the local social services department are taking out care proceedings to have the children fostered because of Karen's limitations as a parent and the extremely disturbed behaviour of the children. The report to the court explained all this but because it is her third conviction, it seems the court gave her community service as a punishment!'

After some discussion the team agreed that Karen would appear to be most suitable for a single placement and Mike was to approach MENCAP for a potential placement as a volunteer working in their day centre. Gina was to telephone social services and inform them of Karen's involvement on a community service order and ask them for an appropriate child minder for Karen's children whilst she carried out the community service work.

This led on to a debate about new guidelines for community service individual placements and the Unit's requirement to increase their hours worked on such placements to 20% from last years figures of 7.5%. These placements are not universally popular with community service staff who feel that standards are more difficult to sustain when supervision is not carried out directly. They are also seen as a cheap option, since no paid supervisors are needed.

However, the main reason for increasing individual placements was not financial but a firmly held belief that they directly involved the community in supervising its offenders and also that they were far more rewarding for the offender because they offered interesting work opportunities and provided the offender with trust and responsibility. Brian's appointment had been partly to cover the need to increase individual placements as well as to cover the increase in work from the Criminal Justice Act 1991. Supported by Brian and Mike, Gina explained that there were a number of important priorities in organising good quality placements which were outlined in the practice guidelines and if carried out should alleviate the worries of those team members who were critical.

'First of all you need clear written information for the host organisation explaining about the community service scheme and its requirements on the offender as well as the expectations of the quality of supervision required by the host agency. The probation service's health and safety and equal opportunities policies also need to be explained alongside information about insurance and liabilities. Once the placement supervisor and any other nominated people understand about community service the next important stage is to take along any prospective offender for a three-way discussion and draw up a contract of attendance, times of work and type of work to be carried out. The last vital element is regular contact between the community service officer and the placement supervisor and offender. On each work date a minimum of a telephone call must be made and once a month a personal visit to see the supervisor, collect the month's time sheet and see the offender to discuss the progress of the placement. Most importantly if the placement host contacts the office for help or advice about the offender we must respond straight away.'

It was agreed that although Brian was responsible for developing individual placements and would take the prime role in liaison it would be the duty community service officer for the day who would take responsibility for visiting and/or telephoning the placement just as they would visit each work party on their duty day. Brian went on to explain that he had widened the scope of placements; they had virtually all been within Aged Person's Homes when he started work but since then he had personally contacted and visited various community groups and had agreements in principal to take on offenders at most of those he had visited.

Brian stressed that he needed to keep this interest going and to place individuals quickly so that the host agency would not become disenchanted with nobody being referred. To this end, Brian and Mike had produced a display board with photos and details of every available placement. This would be on display in the waiting room and at the initial interview it would be helpful if the community service officers could get an idea from the offender if they were interested in any of the placements and then pass on the details of the interested person to Brian.

Some of the more interesting placements Brian had developed were in the local WRVS clothing store helping to sort out and provide clothes, bedding etc; assisting in the Oxfam shop either serving or helping to sort out the donations; a placement at the RSPCA kennels working with the staff looking after the animals; a place at the local riding school for the disabled helping the disabled people to ride but also looking after the animals; in conjunction with Mike there were now placements available at the West Indian Community Centre helping to prepare for the carnival as well as working in the coffee bar and drop-in centre; a placement in the Asian Community Centre; work on the transport scheme for the elderly/disabled and the day centre for physically disabled people, helping individuals with various crafts and projects.

After a discussion on lost and damaged tools (a recurring problem) the last item involved Gina explaining to the team that a new order involved a young man named Carl Conrad, whose offences involved making obscene phone calls and an indecent assault. It was agreed that he had such potential to re-offend that he would work his whole order at the workshop where he could be controlled in a safe environment. Ted Bowen, the workshop manager had successfully dealt with Carl on a previous order and could supervise him closely.

On Saturday there were newly appointed magistrates visiting the scheme to see how it actually operated.

'The visit will be for half a day from 10.00 until 1.00', Gina explained and said the format would be: 'I'll talk to them for an hour about those people most suitable for community service orders, the National Standards we work to, the standard of supervision, the types of work we undertake and then the enforcement procedures, including our policy on breaches in court. After that Mike and I will then take them in one of the minibuses around some of our current ongoing and also recently completed projects.'

Monday afternoon

On Monday afternoon George went to see about the paint drip at Minnie Brown's home. And it got worse. Minnie was extremely apologetic as she didn't want any fuss but there were runs on all the window panes and paint splashes on the carpet, whilst half of a door had been missed. The problem was compounded as far as Minnie was concerned because the group had left at 2.00 pm and she felt sure they could have tidied up. George assured Minnie that they would have a team round to tidy up and the whole matter would be investigated.

'But I don't want to get him into trouble. He was such a lovely man,' Minnie concluded.

Meanwhile Gina was having problems obtaining a suitable childminder for Karen Macinlay. The social worker involved in the case was grateful for the information about the community service order but insisted that none of their registered childminders had got the expertise to be able to control such difficult children as Karen's! After further phone calls to the senior social worker and the area officer, Gina had finally contacted the Day Care Organiser who was hopeful that one of her day carers, who provided support to families who were not coping, might be able to help.

Projects

The Corporate Plan for last year, besides increasing individual placements, had also given the team the target of working on a wider variety of projects. These included 'people' projects (both for individuals and groups), environmental tasks, work for voluntary groups and crime prevention projects. The team had worked hard to get a variety of interesting and stimulating tasks.

Work parties revolved around some ongoing regular projects, which carried on every week; then there were longer term projects which would be completed in the future and other short projects for just a single, or a few days. The fixed projects and longer term projects were generally allocated to a particular supervisor who was the consistent factor for that project.

The other 'one off' projects were shared between the rest of the 'pool' of supervisors so that each supervisor was regularly offered work, but not necessarily every week.

Jane and Mike were ringing around the agreed supervisors to ask them if they wanted to work on particular days that week.

Ted Bowen was the only full time supervisor. Ted took work parties in the workshop for the three weekdays and had a work party each Saturday helping to renovate a community centre in a run down area of Dowerin. The workshop was predominantly involved in making wooden items and some furniture restoration. Some of the wood was donated by a large local manufacturer of kitchen equipment who gave the workshop their unwanted wood. The other main source was recycled wood from the furniture collection scheme run by the probation office. Any old furniture that was collected that could not be re-distributed or repaired in the workshop was broken up and the wood cleaned up for re-use. The workshop made signs, stiles and footpath signs for the National Park rangers, wooden toys for nurseries, notice boards, picnic tables, bird tables, bat boxes, fencing and basically anything from wood which might be needed by the community.

Ted's other project in the community centre involved a range of building skills, bricklaying, plastering, concreting, woodworking as well as painting and decorating.

On Friday, Ted's other work day, he planned his work for the workshop as well as completing small jobs which did not need or could not take a full work party. He usually had one offender working as his assistant and regularly used Fridays to put security locks and spy holes in the homes of vulnerable elderly people referred by Age Concern. This project involved the local Crime

127

Prevention police officers who provided these security devices from donations by a national security firm and also financial contributions by the local Crime Prevention Panel.

The other ongoing projects for the Dowerin team were a weekly 'Bag Run' for Help the Aged and Oxfam. One week, a team labelled and then took out black dustbin liners which were distributed to houses in an area of the city and then, the following week, collected them with any goods donated by the householder. This project was carried out alternately for the two charities. Throughout the year a team also maintained and grew produce on an allotment which was part of the grounds of a local hostel for homeless ex-offenders. This was jointly run by the hostel and the community service unit with the hostel staff supervising individual offenders working on the allotment on some days and work parties being involved when winter digging and other labour intensive tasks were needed. The produce which was grown was split between the hostel and Age Concern for distribution to elderly people. The other two on-going projects were the 'Forth Road Bridge' job at a huge local church and community centre which involved community service in a one day per week maintenance of the painting of the centre; the second, maintenance of the grounds and the painting and decorating of a large old country house run by a charitable trust on the outskirts of Dowerin which provided temporary shelter for homeless single parents and their children.

Another scheme which had operated for over two years involved a team visiting a large residential home for the elderly on one evening per week and spending two hours playing various games such as bingo, dominoes and crib with the elderly residents. When people are interviewed prior to starting a new order—if the individual presents any trade or other skills or talents, or particular interests—then an attempt is made to match them with the available work. For example, a painter and decorator could be slotted into the 'Forth Road Bridge' church project although they might have to start on another work party until a vacancy in the church project team became available.

The 'one off' projects would take up the rest of the community service workers who did not have work preferences or whose orders were only short. This generally involved clearing gardens in the summer for individual elderly, handicapped or single parents who lived in their own homes; in the winter more painting and decorating jobs for individuals in the community are carried out although some of these painting and decorating jobs are always tackled throughout the year. There are also various other interesting 'one off' jobs which operate during the week.

With such a range of tasks and placements available the team hope to match an individual's skills with a relevant task right at the beginning of the order but there is also the scope to move individuals between projects if they show particular abilities during the period of the order.

$$\bullet\bullet\bullet\bullet\bullet$$

Tuesday

Besides the regular work parties on Tuesday, Ted has two interesting 'one off' jobs. In the morning, he is taking his team to a local junior school to pick up two benches which have been vandalised and these will be repaired at the workshop.

Mike spotted this in an article in the local paper and contacted the school who were delighted that offenders were actually going to repair the benches.

Ted is then going on from the workshop with his team to put up the finished articles they have been working on for some weeks. The team have been making poles with cross-members at the top and inserting imitation foxes' eyes. These 'foxes' will be placed in the woods and bushes alongside the busy A362 to frighten the wild deer away from the road. Many have been killed by speeding cars at night. The foxes' eyes should help to protect both the deer and the motorists.

The first major incident of the week occurred on Tuesday afternoon when Jane took a phone call from Bill Fielding who was working with a party of five at the church and community centre.

'Can you come out here now please, Jane. I have got a problem with some money disappearing from the church's souvenir shop', said Bill. Within ten minutes Jane had reached the church to find Bill in one of the side rooms with the whole group. He explained to Jane, 'We have been working in the foyer painting the walls and skirting board near the souvenir table. The verger counted up the takings and float after lunch and there is £20 missing. He was not there all morning as there had only been a few visitors. Obviously we are all under suspicion.' After some conferring Bill and Jane agreed on a course of action and Jane addressed the group. 'You all realise that this could be very serious and if the money is not found the verger has said he will call the police. This means we will all have to wait here and the police will want to interview and possibly search all of you, including Bill.'

'Now, if it is one of this group the verger has said he will take no further action if the money is "found". So Bill and I are going to have a search around outside the foyer to see if we can find the money. In a few minutes we will go and see the verger and get him to come back and check the till again. Do you all understand what I am saying?' Nods from the group and as Bill and Jane left, Bill turned and said, 'of course if no-one here was involved then there is nothing to hide and no reason to be worried'. The verger returned after about 15 minutes with Jane and Bill and although the till was still empty Bill spotted some money down the back of the books displayed in front of the till. Bill and Jane went back into the side room and announced the good news that the money had been found and that the party would carry on with the work.

Later on in the day, in confidence, one of the party had told Bill he couldn't side with anyone stealing from a church and said that in future they ought to be careful where they put Shane Scott to work but if challenged, he would deny saying anything to Bill at all.

Jane returned to the office and recounted all this to Gina. It was agreed that it would be on the agenda at next week's meeting. Shane did have previous convictions for theft and was out of work and although there was no actual proof, Gina believed it would be safer for all concerned if Shane worked on outdoor projects in the future. But equally they would have to keep a watchful eye on all the group members.

129

Wednesday

On Wednesday the luncheon club operates and this week—after the lunch—seven of the elderly residents with the supervisor and a party of four offenders are to visit a stately home.

On Wednesday mornings Gina attends the regular weekly court session which deals with breaches of orders supervised by the probation service. Some months previously, after much effort and negotiation, John Sleeman and the local courts team had managed to persuade the magistrates' courts that a separate probation breach court would be more economic and efficient, especially as the Criminal Justice Act 1991 and National Standards might produce more breaches of community orders and prison licences. After one or two initial teething problems the breach court had been accepted and seemed to have raised the awareness of all concerned of the importance of this kind of work.

On this particular day, Gina had eight people listed for breach although only four people actually attended and one of the summonses had been returned marked 'not known at this address'—a not unusual phenomenon! On the first occasion an individual was breached on their community service order, as long as they indicated some interest and commitment to completing their order, the probation officer would ask for a nominal penalty for the breach—between £10 and £50 if a fine was considered or, if the person had outstanding fines or very limited income, then some extra community service hours and the order to continue. If there was some uncertainty about the individual's likelihood of carrying out the order then the magistrates would be asked to adjourn for a period of a few weeks to test out the person's commitment. Equally if a person had only a few work shifts left then these dates would be stated in open court and the case adjourned until just after the last work date. If someone refused to complete their order then the application would be to have the order revoked and the person re-sentenced. This was also the normal agreed procedure for a second breach—only if there were particularly unusual circumstances would the officer ask for the order to continue after a second breach.

This policy seemed to provide much more uniform, consistent and fair practice across the county and the number of orders successfully completed had actually increased. However the breach court could be quite hectic and tiring. Gina had to interview each of the four people who had attended and do some quick planning so as to use this time to interview and to motivate each of them to finish their order. Then Gina presented the case. Each person who was to continue with the order was asked to confirm in their own words to the court the agreement that had been reached as to their responsibility for completing their community service hours. Gina had certainly found that this had a positive impact on future attendance!

The only case which did not come into these guidelines today was an individual who had been providing sick notes for some months and who now had an appointment to see a neurological consultant because of severe headaches and dizziness. The court adjourned the matter and asked for the consultant to be contacted about a diagnosis. Gina believed that this would result in an application for revocation as she did not feel the man would ever be fit enough to complete his order.

George had been following up the Minnie Brown affair and on his way home had called round to see Len North, the supervisor.

The gist of the conversation was that Len, who appeared genuinely surprised at the fuss, was adamant that he had explained to Minnie, who could be forgetful and often got confused, that he had run out of paint for the door and had no turps or carpet cleaner but he would get these for next week and return to tidy up all the jobs. Len had said that by 2.00 pm he had had quite enough of the two difficult lads in such a confined space and the third had finished his hours and his order. So, given that he had no more materials he finished early at Minnie's and went to a garden around the corner which he had worked on last week and had a bonfire with the left over rubbish that would have dried out.

'Well why didn't you put all this on your work sheet?' said George who was furious as this was not the first time Len had gone off to do his own thing. 'And how were we going to get the paint and turps if you did not tell us?' George went on to explain how much trouble had been caused and the loss of goodwill with Age Concern by Len's unthinking behaviour. 'I will have to take this back to the team and Gina and John Sleeman will have to decide what to do. But in the meantime, I will expect you to finish off the job properly at Minnie's this weekend. I will call and tell her that you are going to clean up and finish the painting on Saturday'.

• • • • •

Thursday

The 'one off' job for Thursday is clearing an overgrown footpath for a local parish council which has responsibility for maintenance but no money and no workers. Local people have complained that the path is frightening in its present overgrown state because of the potential dangers of hidden assailants.

The same work team also have a set of 'Neighbourhood Watch' signs to put up on designated lampposts in that area.

Brian had called in to see the manager of MENCAP. Sam 'Sunny' Miller was one of Brian's most positive contacts in Dowerin. Sunny was very pro-community service after some excellent work last year when community service workers had dug out the foundations, laid a concrete base and erected a pre-fabricated office extension to the MENCAP building and then landscaped the ground around the office. Sunny seemed to have contacts in most statutory and voluntary agencies and as an Afro-Caribbean he had helped Brian by introducing him to many people who Sunny thought might help to provide individual placements. Brian was grateful as they had led to some successful placements for black offenders in their own ethnic community groups.

Brian explained to Sunny about Karen Macinlay's community service order and arranged to bring Karen down to see Sunny next Tuesday for a three-way meeting to see if Karen and the MENCAP centre would be a mutually compatible placement.

• • • • •

131

Friday

On Friday only Gina and Brian, who was the duty community service officer covering the weekend, were at work. Gina had five interviews during the day and Brian spent most of the day organising materials, tools and work sheets for the weekend as well as calling at the local town centre junior school to confirm that the deputy head would meet Gina and Mike and the magistrates tomorrow morning to show them the plans and explain about the project starting next week to develop the allotment and garden from disused/derelict land at the school. Both the school and the community service unit wanted to get good public relations from the project and there was also a large scale article about the scheme being published the following week in the local paper.

Gina's first three interviews were with community service workers who had two unacceptable failures and would be breached if they recorded a third. The interviews were part of the process to try and ensure people completed their order. Gina certainly thought that her social work skills were important in these interviews. She found that they generally took the form of helping those who were having genuine difficulties or personal problems or alternatively threatening, cajoling or stimulating those who were disinterested and unmotivated into attending for work. Inevitably many did not take the opportunity to come in and see her and only one of the first three did attend. This was a seventeen-year-old young man who had recently been kicked out of home and was sleeping rough in a lean-to in a local wood. Gina made an appointment for him with the probation service accommodation officer for later that morning and suspended him from the scheme for next week's work appointment. If they had managed to get him somewhere to live he could re-start his community service work the following week. The fourth appointment involved a nineteen-year-old Asian community service worker who had been sent home by George for being late. The young man complained in the interview that George was picking on him because he was black and that another white community service worker had walked in just in front of him and been allowed to work. On showing the young man his work record it was obvious that it had been his third time late for work and he had been given the benefit of the doubt on the first occasion and had had half an hour taken off his time for the second.

Gina said, 'Although it was right to send you home, I will find out about the circumstances of the other person being allowed to work and ask what happened. I will see you next week at the same time to discuss what is going to happen after I have looked into the whole matter.' Another job for next week, thought Gina. The last appointment also did not turn up but another medical certificate from him had arrived in the post that morning. Gina had asked to see him particularly to talk to him about the continuing sick notes and the possibility of a second medical opinion and potential revocation of the order. That will have to be a home visit next week, Gina noted in her diary. Before her last interview Gina telephoned the social services day carer who had been recommended and arranged to take Karen and her three children round to see her next Tuesday morning before Karen's appointment at MENCAP.

Gina then worked through all the permanent record sheets of each community service order to check that all were being worked and that all details of following up failures and absences had been noted. This was a regular Friday routine before the team meeting on Monday—a vital cog in the weekly system.

• • • • •

The weekend
The visits by the magistrates seemed to be very successful. They all made positive comments about the scheme and how interesting they had found the trip. The majority said that they had been impressed by how well organised the scheme was run but above all, they were most impressed by the sheer amount of high quality work which was being carried out by offenders for those people in the community who most needed help but could least afford it. Magistrates liked the variation of work projects which provided for all areas of the community and the fact that the jobs did actually involve physically or emotionally demanding work. This was seen as a punishment to the offender as they had to give up at least one day per week of their time to work hard for other people. In particular they had all been positive about the 'partnership' with the police in relation to the Saturday 'one off job' which had involved a team putting car crime prevention leaflets on each car in all the town centre car parks. Both this project and the erecting of 'Neighbourhood Watch' signs had come out of a recent meeting between Gina, Brian and the two local crime prevention police officers.

The weekend also brought its share of individual satisfactions. Two housebound eighty-year-olds, extolling the virtues of the four robust and heavily tattooed young men (with numerous convictions) who were decorating for them; an offender who had finished a placement at an old people's home being offered paid work there as a care assistant; even a community service worker with a severe alcohol problem who had managed to survive another lunchtime break without needing a drink . . . These are the counterbalance to the failures and the disappointments and the offenders who have to be returned to court. In short— they are the reasons for starting all over again, next week.

Chapter 9 Where Next? Future Developments in Community Service

John Crawforth

To predict the future of any community-based sanction in the present criminal justice climate is a hazardous task. The early 1990s have seen a level of turbulence in the criminal justice system and in public reaction to crime which is probably unmatched in the post-war period. Major organisational changes have taken place in the magistrates' courts, the Crown Prosecution Service and the prison system. Radical proposals for an overhaul of the legal profession are being matched by an equally far-reaching scrutiny of police force organisation. The report of the Royal Commission on the operation of the criminal justice system is likely to produce significant recommendations. Controversy surrounded the Criminal Justice Act 1991 within its first few months of operation and amendments to it were made.

Against this uncertain background, the community service order, now 20 years old and a relatively well-established option within the sentencing framework, has enjoyed a resurgence whilst the use of some other community sentences seems to have ebbed away. Evidence for this at the time of writing is far from conclusive but early indications are that of the range of community-based measures open to the courts—a range widened by the Criminal Justice Act 1991—the community service order is gaining the continued approval of sentencers and an expanding share of the market.

If this is so, what are the reasons for it? Will community service prove to have an enduring appeal to sentencers and where are the ingredients of this? Can the use of the community service order go on expanding or will some natural 'plateau' be reached? What are the implications of continued growth for the organisation of the probation service which administers the scheme? What are the key challenges for managers and practitioners in developing community service and what are the main weaknesses that have been exposed by two decades of experience? What threats and what opportunities lie ahead for community service and how might it look twenty years from now?

Learning from the past

Before looking forward, we first need to understand something of the story so far, to examine some of the features of the order's undoubted success and some of the difficulties and dilemmas which have hindered its progress.

The history of the community service order will already be familiar to many readers and is charted elsewhere in this book (see *Chapters 1* and *2*). It is worth remembering, however, just how effectively community service established itself within a few years of its experimental introduction in six probation areas in 1973. In 1974 it represented just 0.3% of the total number of sentences given for all indictable offences but by 1984 this figure had risen to 7.5%. By 1991, community service orders accounted for 10% of all sentences passed for indictable offences and 13% in the Crown Court.

This level of growth had immediate implications for the recruitment of staff by the probation service, particularly to the ancillary grade. In effect it created a new workforce. A report, 'Community Service in the 80s' (1) published by the Association of Chief Officers of Probation in June 1987 noted that whereas the numbers of senior probation officers and probation officers working in community service grew by 10% between 1981 and 1985 the number of ancillary staff increased by 67%. Whilst the rate of growth has slowed down since, the 1980s saw a continued expansion of staff employed in community service schemes and produced changes in the probation service's organisational structure and personnel requirements which could scarcely have been anticipated a decade earlier.

A review of community service by the Prison Reform Trust (2) in June 1983 concluded that:

'Almost uniquely amongst penal sanctions, it appears to be universally accepted that community service by offenders is beneficial. It has provided sentencers with a positive and cost-effective sentence which appeals to all strands of penological thinking. It allows offenders to make some amends for their offences and contributes to the public good'.

This confident assessment was reinforced in a Council of Europe document (3) which described community service as:

'. . . probably the most progressive alternative measure introduced in European criminal law in the last ten years, the one which seems to offer the most possibilities and the one which raises the most hopes.' ('Alternative measures to Imprisonment', Council of Europe, 1986).

A special attraction of community service to policy makers during the 1980s was its evident popularity with sentencers when dealing with young adult offenders. By 1986, 44% of all orders made were on those between the ages of 17 and 20 and so community service began to assume critical importance in public debate about how to reduce the rapidly growing numbers of young adults in the prison system.

Its impact in that direction in practice has been much less impressive. Most estimates of the percentage of offenders on community service who have actually been diverted from custody fall in the range 45 to 50% (Willis)(4). This has occurred in spite of the fact that 86% of probation areas responding to the ACOP 'Community Service Survey', published in 1987, viewed community service as '. . . either a strict alternative to custody or, at least, a high tariff disposal'. The fact that community service orders have held an unclear and ambiguous position within the range of sentences on offer to the court has been much written about

135

and this is not the place to rehearse those arguments. A key point for the future is that criminal justice legislation is given practical effect by hundreds of daily, individual sentencing decisions and that the demands and needs of the judiciary can not necessarily be constrained by the probation service taking a particular policy stance, unless that stance is firmly rooted in the legislation itself. The experience of community service in this respect should provide some clear pointers in the current debate about the use and standing of the combination order—an issue I want to return to later.

The history of community service has been one of managing diversity. Here, too, the probation service has learned some important lessons which should have a bearing on the future of the scheme. In the early phases of its development, even from the time of the six experimental schemes, marked differences appeared in the criteria for assessing offender suitability, the type and range of work undertaken and the way in which individual schemes were organised, whether on a centralised or de-centralised basis. Whilst complete uniformity between 55 probation areas would have been an unattainable and undesirable objective, the rapid pace of development and the individual preferences of service managers and staff led to a range of practice which attracted increasingly adverse comment and began to throw some doubt on the credibility of community service. A study of the schemes (5) operating in a northern city and an eastern county in the late 1980s identified some common practices but also found a remarkable amount of diversity. These were present:

'. . . in a variety of aspects, particularly the unit organisation and involvement of main-grade probation staff in the day-to-day functioning of the scheme; the recruitment, background, role and terminology of the community service officer; the importance allocated to assessment of suitability and the role of the social enquiry report, the proportional use of single placements; and very different standards relating to . . . the breach process.' (Skinns 1990)

Pre-occupied by other concerns some probation managers may have failed to register the mounting concern in government circles that community service had lost its way, that it had become an 'easy option' characterised by undemanding tasks, poor quality supervision and inconsistent enforcement. Much of the evidence for these judgments may have been anecdotal and it certainly stood in contrast to the courts' increasing use of community service for more serious offences. By 1986 11% of all orders were made for offences of violence against the person compared with 6% a decade earlier; the proportion of orders made for theft and handling offences fell from 46% to 39% over the same period. Nonetheless, the Home Office announced in May 1988 that community service would in future be subject to national standards which would provide an opportunity:

'. . . for the probation service to show that community service can be operated throughout the country to the high standards of the best.' (6)

Alongside the Criminal Justice Act 1991, National Standards have been applied to many aspects of probation work but the choice of community service as the initial area for their introduction caused some surprise and not a little consternation at the time.

To summarise this brief review, community service has made a remarkable impact on the criminal justice scene in just a few years; has offered a radical new option to sentencers and changed beyond recognition the way in which the probation service operated within the community. But it has not all been plain sailing. As could have been anticipated, no new sentence could have developed so rapidly without throwing up a range of fresh problems and dilemmas. Some of these have faded into history—for example the interminable debates about community service as an 'alternative to custody' or 'sentence in its own right' and the frequent attempts to relate the length of an order to the period of imprisonment it might replace. But whilst the advent of the Criminal Justice Act 1991 and its sentencing principles radically changes the debate many of the issues emerging in the first 20 years of the scheme remain current. The questions posed are more pressingly in need of an answer. Community service in an era of cash-limits for the probation service (and magistrates' courts), market-testing and compulsory competitive tendering will also face new challenges. The need to ensure compliance with equal opportunities and to eliminate discriminatory practice from all aspects of probation work will make new demands on community service—demands it must meet if it is to justify the good faith that many place in it. What these challenges may be and how the probation service might respond forms the subject of the remainder of this chapter.

Community service and community sentencing

The Criminal Justice Act 1991 marks a watershed in the development of penal policy by placing community-based measures at the heart of sentencing, restricting the circumstances in which custody may be used and establishing the principle of graduated restriction on liberty. Whilst a wide range of community penalties are capable of restricting an individual offender's freedom, community service embodies the principles of the Act in their clearest form. It does this for two simple reasons. Firstly, as a penalty (unlike the probation order) it is measured in hours and is, in effect, a 'fine on time'; secondly, the hours awarded are capable of continuous gradation between the minimum and maximum limits in order to reflect the seriousness of the case. Whilst these features of community service are self-evident, together they ensure that of all the community-based options which pre-dated the Criminal Justice Act 1991, community service translates most readily and naturally to the sentencing principles enshrined in the Act. It emerges, therefore, as a measure which is central to the extension of community sentencing and which can and should be capable of enlarging its share of the market.

The success of any penal measure depends very largely on the extent to which it can be seen by sentencers and the general public to have a specific, unambiguous purpose which distinguishes it from other sentences and enables it to meet a need which they do not. Community service to date has been popular with sentencers because of its straightforward, uncomplicated appeal and the fact that it is the most visible and tangible of all probation managed disposals. And yet despite all these advantages its progress has been hampered by confusion over its primary purpose and the sentencing philosophy that underpins it. The challenge for the probation service now is to promote and articulate clearly what the primary purpose of community service should be. This needs to be done in the context of the new sentencing philosophy which the courts must embrace. The probation service will need to ensure that it does not define this unilaterally and expect the courts to follow suit—it would be futile to repeat the mistakes of the 'alternative to custody' versus 'sentence in its own right' debate. Any worthwhile re-assertion of a clear purpose for community service can only emerge from open dialogue between the service, sentencers and other participants in the criminal justice process. Proper attention should be given to how far notions of reparation, deterrence—and even rehabilitation—have any relevance for community service within the new sentencing framework. Proponents of the order have claimed at various stages that it meets the requirements of each but its raison d'etre must surely now be more tightly defined. This must centre upon the provision of a constructive penalty which first and foremost restricts liberty as required by the seriousness of the offence. It in no way prevents the scheme from being operated in an imaginative way with attention to varied work placements and a high quality service—it does recognise honestly and openly that the community service order operating in a 'just deserts' context is primarily a retributive measure and will be seen by most sentencers as such.

With this challenge to achieve greater clarity about community service comes a real opportunity. Though the penalty aspect of the order lies in its ability to deprive an offender of his or her free time, the work done must be purposeful, socially worthwhile and make demands on the person carrying it out, whether physical or psychological. Community service schemes throughout the country have developed work placements that meet these criteria and in doing so recognised that it is not just sufficient to restrict liberty. The time captured in this way has to be re-directed to 'add value' to the community and the nature of the work done is critical to whether the courts have confidence in community service and use it. It is, in other words, not good enough to take time away from offenders and leave it at that. National Standards and, indeed, common sense require that activity undertaken should generally stretch and challenge the offender, not be dull, routine and undemanding.

The revised National Standards issued in August 1992 emphasise this point and helpfully underline that the main purpose of the community service order '. . . is to re-integrate the offender into the community'. Whilst re-integration is not the same as rehabilitation (defined by the CJA 1991 as a statutory purpose of the probation order and the probation element in a combination order) it is made clear that by involving offenders constructively with the local community, the service has a valuable opportunity 'to promote the rehabilitation of offenders generally' (7) (para 4, p 67).

Community service, perhaps unique amongst the sentences open to courts, meets the prevailing concerns of the courts that if they are to use community-based options more frequently they want re-assurance that there will be an impact on the lives of offenders and that this will be visible to the wider public.

These National Standards, rightly regarded by many in the probation service as a significant improvement on the 1989 version, provide a framework for consistent practice. But they must amount to more than an expression of hope. The Association of Chief Officers of Probation report 'Community Service Orders: Monitoring National Standards', July 1991 (8) suffered from a number of limitations but concluded that there was little evidence of the 1989 standards achieving consistent management or practice and that 'considerable variations remain both between and within services' (p 69). Service managers must expect that they will be called on to demonstrate that the requirements of National Standards are being met in their own areas and standards are, after all, not just a basis for good practice but a framework for accountability. An HM Inspectorate Report, published in July 1992, stresses that:

'Services should urgently develop arrangements to monitor local and national standards of practice. These will ensure that information vital to the maintenance of practice is continuously available to line managers, enabling them to exercise more immediate influence over those directly responsible for service delivery than findings of inspections will allow them to do.' (9)

This may be a laudable enough aim but if the service is to develop effective monitoring systems of this kind across the whole range of work covered by National Standards the implications are enormous. Some realism needs to be injected into the debate about just how far area-wide monitoring systems can be developed before the introduction of a nationally agreed case management system which will allow much of this information to be captured routinely, using computer applications. Nor should it be forgotten that evidence of compliance with national standards only takes us so far. They are essentially a limiting framework. My own recent experience of training more than 200 magistrates in the Lancashire Probation Area confirms that they are just as interested, if not more so, in how standards convert into reality—with how the scheme *actually* works in practice, with the kind of work available locally and how decisions on enforcement get taken by real community service staff in the course of their daily work.

Community service and the combination order
Many of the points made about the need for clarity of purpose can be related equally to the combination order, a new form of community sentence introduced in the Criminal Justice Act 1991. It allows a period of one to three years probation to be combined with 40 to 100 hours community service. Its statutory purpose is partially defined in section 11(2) of the 1991 Act as:

—to secure the rehabilitation of the offender;
—to protect public from harm from the offender; and/or
—to prevent the offender from committing further offences.

In other words, the probation element has the same statutory purpose as the probation order. Does this imply that it is really a probation order with an additional community service element, as available under existing Scottish legislation; or are the probation and community service elements really of equal

139

standing? If they are, why is this not reflected in the wording of the Act?

However these questions are answered, ambiguity has certainly surrounded the introduction of the new order. Nor has it had a very good press within the probation service. During the consultation stage on the Criminal Justice Bill the combination order received a lot of critical comment from service organisations. Attempts were made to persuade the Home Office either to abandon their proposals altogether or to confine the new sentence to the Crown Court, on the basis that it would prove to be the most demanding and onerous of the community sentences available. The basis for this was not always clear. Why, for example, is a combination order of one year's probation and 40 hours community service necessarily more onerous than a community service order of 240 hours? Though it would be far too simplistic to compare probation and community service orders only on the basis of the hours involved, a community service order of maximum length represents a much greater deprivation of liberty than a combination order which includes the minimum periods of probation and community service allowed by the legislation. In the example above, the probation element in the combination order would need to deprive offenders of four hours of their time each week before the restriction of liberty equalled that of a 240 hour community service order. This is hardly likely in practice, even under the most exacting interpretation of National Standards. Of course it will be argued that there is a qualitative difference, that the demands made on an offender during their supervision by the probation officer will be of a different order. They will find their attitudes challenged, their motivation probed, their offending behaviour under attack. In the best of probation practice all of this may be true but will the offender always find probation supervision so exacting, the experience so much more onerous than a demanding community service placement? And even if the offender does, will the distinction always be so apparent to a court? The onus is on the probation service to make out the case.

Having failed to deter the Government from introducing the combination order or restricting its use to the Crown Court, the probation service has been left with something of a dilemma. Unenthusiastic about the new order it has fastened on to the compromise wording of the National Standards—that the combination order will be appropriate for 'amongst the most serious offenders given a community sentence' and in practice used most often in the Crown Court. In some probation areas magistrates have been encouraged not to make Combination Orders, in others service managers have urged staff not to propose the order in reports for the magistrates' court. This has not gone down well. Apart from the obvious irritation some sentencers have expressed at being effectively denied an option that the new legislation gives them, there is little sign that the utterances of the probation service have had any impact on actual sentencing practice. There are loud echoes here of the previous enjoinders to courts to use community service only as an alternative to custody—an essentially unpopular message which sentencers frequently ignored because the legislation did not require this, nor did it correspond with their view of community service.

Monitoring of the first few months of the combination order by the ACOP Community Service Committee revealed that magistrates were in fact using the new order far more often than the Crown Court: around 75% of combination orders were being made in the magistrates' courts. More worryingly, from a probation service viewpoint, in most cases orders were made despite the lack of a clear proposal to that effect in the pre-sentence report. Courts, in other words, were making combination orders without being advised by the probation service that they were the most suitable option or that there was a satisfactory prospect of completion.

Clearly there is some work for the probation service to do here. The challenge for service managers and staff is not to retreat into irritation with sentencing behaviour nor to adopt inflexible views about how courts should behave but to accept the appeal of the combination order to sentencers and work with them to define positively when it should be used. A good starting point would be that courts can use the combination order appropriately when their sentencing requirements cannot be met by either a probation order or community service order made on its own. Though courts must ultimately be the arbiters of offence seriousness and suitability, it is essential in my view that they are satisfied that an offender has a reasonable prospect of completing a combination order. Only the pre-sentence report can properly advise on that and in its absence courts would be operating in hazardous territory. But sentencers must feel confident that probation officers will consider the combination order alongside other options and not hold back from proposing it because of vague, ideological objections.

In fact there is much to be gained from the probation service dropping its initial hostility to the new order. Supervision of the combination order holds out real prospects of integrating the work of probation officers and community service officers far more closely than ever before. If the mistrust, suspicion and resentment about status differentials between the two groups reported in a number of research studies (10), (5) (Vass, 1984; Skinns, 1990); are to be overcome how better to do this than through co-operative effort in the supervision of a single order? If community service needs to be firmly integrated within the service's work—and I would argue that it does—then to ignore the potential benefits of the combination order would be to miss a real opportunity.

Reflecting on the history of community sentences at this point it is hard not to be struck by a peculiar paradox. In the early 1970s the probation service was a reluctant convert to community service. Many people within the service opposed the new order on the grounds that it was at odds with the 'social work tradition' of the service and lacked any rehabilitative component. Twenty years further on when the combination order provides both reparation to the community and an opportunity to address the offender's needs, the probation service is again unenthusiastic. This is unfortunate, puzzling to sentencers who are being urged to make more use of community sentences and suggests that the service does not always take enough care to see itself as others see it.

Community service and external relations: managing the boundary

The way in which the probation service promotes and manages community service (and combination orders) is a critical part of its future external relations policy. The successful introduction of the community service order has done more than anything else to change the public face of the probation service. It has overcome much of its previous diffidence and developed a more confident and articulate voice on matters which are now continuously in the public arena—crime, sentencing and crime prevention. To link that change directly to the development of community service would be to over-simplify and to neglect many other significant changes which have taken place. Nonetheless for any organisation to project itself effectively to a wider public it must develop a sense of its own worth, its own distinctive contribution. It must have its successes.

From the mid-1970s, community service began to flourish within an organisation which in other respects appeared to be losing its way. A relentless critique of the rehabilitative ethic and mounting evidence (much of it now discredited) that probation intervention did little to halt offending behaviour or deal with its underlying causes left many in the service demoralised. The decline of the probation order seemed terminal and whether the service had a future beyond its work in prisons and in the civil courts began to be questioned. But while some members of the service were lost in introspection others were making radical changes. The first generation of community service organisers were developing a range of imaginative schemes to change the public perception of offenders and what they could achieve. Instead of being the passive recipients of punishment—or even of therapy—they were thrust into an active role and given a chance, as the title of this book reflects, to pay something back.

The probation service, instead of appearing as an organisation with a peculiar pre-occupation for helping those who had committed crimes rather than their victims, began to be seen as one which also cared about the community and which expected offenders to make some positive contribution to it. People who had previously attracted attention only by committing thefts or burglaries, began to appear on television and be featured in the local press working alongside the elderly, the physically handicapped and other vulnerable groups. And it was the probation service that was making this happen. That this caught the public mood and the imagination of the courts is now beyond doubt. There have been many other examples of progressive work done by the probation service in recent years but none quite so immediate, so visible as community service. Of course, the publicity has not all been good. The problem about becoming more public, more open to scrutiny is that your mistakes are there for all to see as well as your achievements. But, taken overall, its success in developing community service has dramatically altered the way in which the probation service is viewed by courts, the wider community and by policy makers. One of the most powerful arguments for keeping community service integrated within probation service work rather than allowing it to develop separately must be the impact that it has made on the service's credibility and self-confidence.

Yet, as any external relations consultant will tell you, publicity should not be a reactive business but a deliberate sustained effort on the part of an organisation to manage its relations with the outside world. For community service to safeguard its future, probation managers must ensure that it is given a central place in their external relations strategy. There is a danger that after the initial 'pioneering' stage an organisation fails to capitalise on the value of an important new development. Recently much time has been consumed by activities which are to do with consolidating the scheme and improving its internal operations. National Standards have been a powerful influence on this.

However worthy all this activity is, there is a danger that community service will become inward-looking, 'systems bound' and will lose the quality of innovation that characterised its early years.

There needs to be some re-investment in public relations activity which draws attention to the impact of community service work and reflects the fact that it is integral to probation's involvement with local communities. A positive re-statement of what offenders can achieve is especially important at the present time when so much of public debate on crime is focused on its negative and harmful aspects. Some of this public relations activity needs to be directed at the wider public and to make use of local and national media channels. Other efforts need to address a different target audience. How well, for example, is community service understood by members of the legal profession, particularly defence lawyers who advocate it on behalf of their clients? Improving their knowledge of how the scheme works in practice should increase the effectiveness of their representation in court and yet too often the probation service regards solicitors and barristers with a wary eye and fails to communicate with them.

At a straightforward level, sentencers often say that their confidence in making a community service order would be greatly increased if they knew exactly what work an offender would be engaged in. In an era when probation officers are being urged to become clearer and more specific in their proposals to court, is it good enough just to indicate that community service is available should the Court want to use it? The logistical problems of being precise about work placements, particularly in Crown Court reports which may be prepared many weeks in advance of the hearing, are well known but has the service done all it can to overcome them? Courts are one of the principle consumers that the probation service has and effective communication with them must be a priority. This leads me to an area in which community service has, I believe, a special contribution to make.

Community service and crime prevention

Community service work can meet a variety of needs and most schemes have a range of projects which, in theory, allow an offender's ability to be matched to a particular work task. The ability to be flexible and responsive about the work to be done is, of course, an important one but too wide a range of activity can produce a fragmented scheme which fails to make a clear impression on the local community. I am not arguing for a narrow, restrictive framework but there is a lot to be said for each scheme having one or two areas of work to which most of its efforts are directed. This not only allows expertise to be built up but enables the scheme's purpose to be more clearly conveyed to the courts and the general public. One such area that demands further attention is the contribution that community service can make to preventing crime.

Opportunities for the probation service here as well as some potential pitfalls are fully described in a recent Home Office report which charts the progress of a 'demonstration project' in Stockport, Greater Manchester (11).

Under the scheme offenders were put to work in renovating a dilapidated community centre on the fringes of a problem estate which had been a constant target for offences of burglary and criminal damage. Apart from the many physical improvements to the centre and its security, the intention was to develop the use of the building by members of the local community including those who had previously offended against it. The wishes of nearby residents were canvassed and a multi-agency steering group set up to oversee the project. With Sports Council funding a high-quality, all-weather, five-a-side football pitch was constructed, largely using community service labour. Other linked projects were carried out in local schools which had also been subject to a high rate of break-ins and vandalism.

In addition to the value of the work done, the scheme had in the words of the report's authors, 'a certain elegance' in re-directing the efforts of offenders to deal with conditions in a local community which were only conducive to more crime. The project had many successes but also delivered some important lessons on the logistics of large-scale community service work, the skill limitations in using offenders as a principle source of labour and on the way such schemes can be integrated within a local community. Implications for the future of community service include the fact that real impact is possible if effort is focused in a particular area, a firm foundation for future partnerships can be laid and courts are receptive to the notion of crime prevention as a legitimate community service activity, particularly where reports contain a specific proposal to that effect. Despite some initial scepticism on the part of community service officers, the project also demonstrated a capacity to motivate staff in working a clearly defined project with a crime prevention objective.

Projects on the scale of the Stockport one would not be easy to replicate in all parts of the country. They are probably only possible where schemes are prepared to take a close look at some of their traditional tasks and to abandon those which have out-lived their usefulness. Where there is a willingness to do this the message is that community service can continue to develop constructive and imaginative ways of putting offenders to work and perhaps do something about crime itself.

Demonstrating effectiveness

Along with other public sector and criminal justice organisations the probation service is increasingly expected to demonstrate that its work has some impact on offending behaviour and that its services are delivered in a cost-effective manner. I want to turn to those two issues as they affect community service and to look at what developments the future may hold.

The last few years have seen a resurgence of interest in whether any particular sentence or method is more effective than others in preventing re-offending. The work done by Gendreau and Ross [12] in particular has given encouragement to practitioners in the service to develop programmes targeted at specific offender groups and to make use of a number of promising methods. In community service, certainly in England and Wales, the debate has been more limited and tended to focus on the overall success rate of community service when set alongside other community disposals. Relatively little attention has been given to whether there are any specific features of community work placements or methods of operation which affect outcomes.

An exception to this has been McIvor's studies [13], [14] of community service schemes in Scotland (1989, 1990) which showed that a relationship did exist between the kind of work placement provided and the successful completion

144

of an order. In brief, she found that successful outcomes were more often associated with individualised placements where the offender was given work in another agency than in group-based work supervised directly by the probation service. Some currently unpublished work by Lloyd and Perry (15) in Manchester throws an interesting light on this. In a study of 106 offenders in one of the community service schemes in Greater Manchester they found that 46% had been subject to action for breach of requirements at some point during the life of the order. They were especially likely to do so in the first 40 hours of the order. They found no statistically significant relationship between breach rates and the age of the offender, their marital status, whether they had a drug or alcohol problem or whether they had been in breach of an order in the past. However, offenders who were employed were more likely to comply with the conditions of their orders than those who were unemployed, presumably, the authors speculate, because they were already adapted to the routine of regular work. Offenders with more serious criminal records were also more likely to be returned to court for breach action than those with few previous convictions or none.

Applying the predictor scale developed by Humphries *et al* to community service they concluded that a high prediction score was much more frequently associated with failure of an order than where the score was low. As in McIvor's study, individualised placements were much more successful, only accounting for 4% of breach action, but on closer examination this seemed to be more to do with careful selection of offenders for individual placements than any specific characteristics of the work done. There was evidence, too, that offenders convicted of 'white-collar' crimes were more likely to be offered individualised placements than those who had not.

This study has a number of important implications for the future. Firstly, that to avoid breakdown more attention needs to be given to induction and supervision in the early stages of an order when failure is more likely. Secondly, that it is possible to identify a 'breach predictor scale' which can be used either to focus on those offenders most likely to relapse or to 'screen out' those who have a very low likelihood of successful completion before an order is made. Thirdly, that within the framework of National Standards more focused intervention by community service staff on those at most risk of failure may pay dividends. The results of Lloyd and Perry's work open up a new agenda for community service managers and may also lead to more effective targeting of the order by courts. This is particularly relevant at a time when many schemes are in danger of being overwhelmed by an influx of new orders made in the months following the introduction of the Criminal Justice Act 1991. The credibility of community service could be easily threatened by a rapid build-up of orders which makes National Standards become difficult to sustain and is reflected in higher rates of breach action for failure to comply.

Another critical issue for the probation service during the 1990s will be to demonstrate that community service schemes as well as other community disposals give value for money. More than two decades ago the Wootton Committee advocated the introduction of community service orders on a number of grounds, including their comparative cheapness. The White Paper, 'Crime Justice and Protecting the Public', published 20 years later, also referred to the

145

importance of costs in the context of using more community-based measures:

'. . . a price cannot be put on justice, but it is not without its costs . . . The most expensive form of punishment is custody. On average it costs £304 a week or £15,800 to keep an offender in custody. 100 hours community service successfully completed costs slightly less than £450 for each offender.'

A study by Knapp, Thomas and Hine (16) in 1990 agreed that community service orders were considerably less costly than custody but that the White Paper figure was misleadingly low and the true cost was probably twice as high. Not only was there a danger that the probation service could not provide community service at the funding level implied by Home Office figures but the true cost was set to rise still higher with the trend towards longer orders and more breach action. As 'market testing' extends throughout the public sector, probation services need to develop more precise ways of costing community service which, to be a true reflection, should include the value added to the community by the work done. Because community service is separately administered and not unlike some work-based schemes already operating in the independent sector, it could be particularly vulnerable to pressure in Government circles to contract out more and more services which have so far been the exclusive preserve of the public sector. If that were to happen it would be an immeasurable loss to the probation service. I have argued that the order has a central place in the range of probation managed disposals, makes a vital contribution to probation service credibility and brings more members of the general public into positive contacts with offenders than any other community sentence. But the probation service cannot afford to be complacent, especially in a policy climate which holds few certainties.

Service managers—and Probation Committees—need to be prepared to fight for its retention on the basis of proven experience and by marshalling the evidence that community service in the hands of the probation service is a cost-effective sanction.

Organising service to the community
Many of the challenges and future possibilities for community service need to be seen in an organisational context. As the opening section of this chapter identified, community service has changed the shape of the probation service. It has brought into the service's employment new staff with different job descriptions, new skills, a wider range of experience and different attitudes to working with offenders. Much of this has been refreshing and has given new impetus to the organisation. But, as a Birmingham University study concluded in 1988 (17):

'The management of community service is perhaps the most complex single task with which the probation service is charged. This not least because of the multiplicity of activities and the variety of actions involved, each with their own set of interests and priorities and their own sources of power and influence. Inevitably, the management of conflict, paradox and uncertainty feature prominently.'

Over 20 years, the principle characteristic of local practice in community service has been its diversity and this has been reflected in organisational and management structures. The ACOP survey 'Community Service in the 80s' (1) found a marked trend towards de-centralised schemes, but with many probation areas retaining some form of central or co-ordinating responsibility. It noted that de-centralisation was aimed at integrating community service with other aspects of the service's work and making it more locally relevant but could sometimes be pursued at the cost of centralised operation which might be more economic, easier to control and more consistent in practice. There was also a worrying degree of variation in the way in which various responsibilities were allocated between probation officer and ancillary grade staff and, indeed, a number of community service schemes functioned (and continue to do so) without any direct probation officer involvement.

Despite the arrival of National Standards the probation service seems to have given limited attention to the organisational implications of delivering consistent, high-quality practice. After two decades of experience, it can surely no longer be good enough simply to record diversity and relate it to variations in the size of probation areas, management structures and geography. Some evidence must have accumulated about management effectiveness and about 'what works' best in organising community service. This is not to imply that any one form of organisation could possibly be superimposed on 55 separate probation areas but can the degree of diversity found between schemes serving similar communities, whether predominantly urban or rural, really be justified?

In the words of a further ACOP study (8) ' . . . many probation services were grappling with similar problems but reaching different solutions, unaware of developments, successes and failures elsewhere. There appears to be an obvious role for ACOP . . . to promote a wider sharing of knowledge.'

Variety of skill and experience amongst staff adds to the vitality of any organisation but if wide differences are allowed to develop between the attitudes and cultures of groups working within the same scheme then problems can be anticipated. In particular, probation services must guard against administrative and ancillary staff feeling under-valued where traditional differentials in pay and conditions of service remain and long-term career development within community service is very much restricted.

Service managers charged with the future developments of the scheme will need to address more vigorously whether the balance of skills and abilities within their organisation is appropriate; whether the historical blend of staff in different grades should be continued; whether the ratio between full-time, part-time, permanent and sessional staff is right. The answers to these questions will in turn have a major impact on how the service develops its personnel and recruitment policies over the next decade.

How well the probation service can resolve many of these dilemmas and grasp the opportunities that lie ahead for community service remains to be seen. It will reflect in turn its ability to prosper in the rapidly changing world of criminal justice. If the first two decades of community service give any indication there must be a lot of cause of hope.

REFERENCES

(1) *Community Service in the 80s,* Association of Chief Officers of Probation (1987), London, ACOP

(2) *Community Service - a guide for Sentencers,* Prison Reform Trust (1983), London, Prison Reform Trust. *Alternative Measures to Imprisonment,* Brussels

(3) *Alternative Measures to Imprisonment,* Council of Europe (1986), Brussels

(4) *Community Service as an alternative to imprisonment: a cautionary view,* Willis, A, Probation Journal, vol 24, 120 to 125

(5) *Community Service Practice,* Skinns, C D (1990), British Journal of Criminology, vol 30, no 1, Winter 1990

(6) Press release to accompany draft of National Standards for Community Service; Home Office (1988), London, HMSO

(7) *National Standards for the Supervision of Offenders in the Community,* Home Office (1992a), London, HMSO

(8) *Community Service Orders: Monitoring National Standards,* Association of Chief Officers of Probation (1991), London, ACOP

(9) *The Development and Implementation of effective arrangements for Internal Monitoring and Inspection in the Probation Service,* Home Office (1992b), London, Home Office

(10) *Sentenced to Labour: Close Encounters with a Prison Substitute,* Vass A, St Ives, Venus Academica

(11) *Community Service and Crime Prevention: The Cheadle Health Project,* Home Office (1992c), Police Research Group, Crime Prevention Unit Series: Paper No 39, London, Home Office Police Department

(12) *Revivication of rehabilitation evidence from the 1980s,* Gendreau, P and Ross, P R (1987), Justice Quarterly, 4, 349 to 407

(13) *Community Service in Scotland: A Summary of the Findings and Conclusions,* McIvor, G (1989), Sterling; Social Work Research Centre, University of Sterling

(14) *Community Service and Custody in Scotland,* McIvor, G (1990), Howard Journal, vol 29 (3), 23 to 31

✕ **(15)** *Community Service—Who Works?,* Lloyd, P M and Perry, N C R (1993), Unpublished

(16) *The Economics of Community Service Orders: A Study of Costs in Five English Areas,* Knapp, M, Thomas, N, Hine, J (1990), Canterbury, Personal Social Services Research Unit, University of Kent

(17) *Study of Community Service Orders: Summary Report,* University of Birmingham (1988), Department of Social Policy and Social Work, University of Birmingham

Chapter 10 Time For Another Big Idea?

Andrew Rutherford

The essays brought together in this volume reflect the considerable presence of the community service order upon the contemporary criminal justice scene (1). The 1970s was a decade of innovation and integration and the 1980s largely one of consolidation and standardisation. As the community service order enters its third decade choices about direction need to be confronted.

In 1970 the proposal by the Advisory Council on the Penal System that there be a community service order was a Big Idea. General notions of community service at home and overseas were much in vogue, and there were some projects in one or two probation areas that reflected something of that spirit. Curiously, there is no detailed record of how the idea was generated within the sub-committee. Barbara Wootton's own account goes no further than saying the sub-committee 'thought up the experiment' (Wootton 1978, p 121). As Roger Hood has noted, while the concept was a response to the idealism of the Community Service Volunteers movement (and the founder of Community Service Volunteers, Alex Dickson, gave evidence to the sub-committee), there was also some similarity with Alexander Paterson's ideology of service which characterised open borstals during the inter-war years (Hood, 1974, p 409, 417).

Probation officers and other criminal justice practitioners were closely involved in discussions with the Wootton sub-committee and helped to fine-tune the recommendations. Indeed, one member of the sub-committee later described the outcome as being a 'negotiated scheme' (Trasler, 1986, p 233). Furthermore a number of probation officers played innovative roles in translating the provisions of the Criminal Justice Act 1972 into practice (see eg, Harding 1974)(2). One of these practitioners has recalled: 'The Wootton Report talked about probation and community service orders as being both punitive and reparative, but also talked about building bridges with local communities which is the term that I hung onto, and I took it as a reconciliatory gesture' (Rutherford, 1993 p78) (3). Unfortunately, this perspective on community service orders has, at least to some extent, been lost sight of in recent years.

Since the early 1980s community service orders became located within the increasingly centralist tenor of criminal policy. Selected as the first aspect of probation service work for the specification of National Standards, Home Office ministers held that orders be rigorous and demanding, with frequent and punctual reporting regarded as part of the discipline experienced by the offender (Home Office 1988, para 2.5). This repackaging of the community service order reflected the prevailing 'culture of severity' (Garland 1989, p 14), but it can also be regarded as a cornerstone of the Criminal Justice Act 1991, serving to present a more strident view of community penalties in their own right and not simply as alternatives to custody. As Andrew Ashworth has commented, the community service order became the plainest example of punishment in the community (Ashworth 1992, p 271).

It does however have to be recognised, that through a successful rearguard action, some chief probation officers were able to blunt the punitive edge to the new National Standards. As one chief probation officer has stated: 'We fought quite a considerable battle to get them rewritten, to allow us more discretion, and I use that discretion quite substantially in running a community service scheme which meets our principles much more than it would if we literally followed the rules' (Rutherford 1993, p 153). Furthermore the revised standards, which accompanied the implementation of the Criminal Justice Act 1991, were further modified so as to be less mechanistic with the intention of helping people through their orders. A challenge for the probation service is to ensure that the Home Office does not gain exclusive hold on setting the direction of policy and practice.

As the community service order enters its third decade it is appropriate to ask whether the probation service is poised for another Big Idea? The political context (which includes the disappearance of bodies such as the Advisory Council on the Penal System) strongly suggests that any such initiative will probably have to come from within the probation service itself. The outline of one way forward is beginning to take shape and encompasses the view of the probation service as a social catalyst which seeks to build bridges to those communities where concerns about crime are most pronounced. One key feature, as suggested by David Mathieson, might be the notion of reparation. Mathieson argued that the probation service, 'still needs convincing of the potential of restorative justice as a concept and its own capacity for turning the concept into practice'. He also proposed that the community service order was the obvious starting point (Mathieson 1992, p 157). However, progress on reparation projects within the probation service has remained tentative and difficult to sustain. In the early 1980s there were a few isolated efforts to form links with victim support groups. One or two pioneers in the restorative justice movement were brought over from North America as consultants but little of this activity was to take root within the probation service (see generally Harding 1987, pp 194 to 208; and Rock 1990, pp 292 to 300) (4).

A more promising strand (and one which John Crawforth highlights in *Chapter 9*) might emerge from a robust reconsideration of the probation service's role in relation to crime prevention. This way forward directly connects with broad aspects of social policy, and as David Garland reminds us, 'constructive, welfare policies of dealing with offenders have the advantage of continually referring us to the wider dimension of the crime problem' (Garland 1989, p 13). Among the issues that arise is the nature of the relationship between the probation service and entities such as the Home Office's Safer Cities programme, and independent organisations such as Crime Concern. A crucial enabling mechanism may lie with new partnership arrangements which are being formed by means of the contracting out powers bestowed on probation committees through the Criminal Justice Act 1991. These emerging structures present imaginative opportunities for the development of community service. By building upon recreational schemes now in place a great deal might be done in terms of work with the ravaged estates and other ills of the urban environment. This direction is not without risk and part of what is required is a reinvention of the ethos of creative risk-taking that characterised the early years of community service. At that time community service staff were the members of the probation service most in touch with their communities. In recent years, the dominance of group activities may have undermined some of that.

One of Britain's more thoughtful commentators has recently argued that the apparatus of criminal justice has become divorced from reality and is largely irrelevant to the problems people are actually facing. Crime, she suggests, is not something that should be left to the police or the courts to deal with in a vacuum but demands constructive measures within the community (Phillips 1993). There are some very real opportunities for the probation service to play a lead role in partnership with the voluntary sector and local government. In this respect the location of probation responsibilities within local government social work departments makes the Scottish scene appear especially promising (McIvor 1992). Developments of this sort carry with them an extension of the probation service's mission but that of course is what happened with the invention of the community service order. On that occasion the promise was one of building bridges to the community but over the years the reality has been to strengthen probation as a correctional arm of the courts. This general viewpoint certainly enjoys some recognition within the probation service. To quote another chief probation officer: 'I would like to think that we are in a bridging position between the fulcrum of the criminal justice system and where the services need to be improved and delivered and built up, which is out in the communities where the vast majority of crime happens, and has to be dealt with, recognising that the courts handle only about five percent of all that.' (Rutherford 1993, p 151). The authors of the Wootton Report anticipated that the details of their Big Idea would be filled in by practitioners (5). The new way forward may emerge incrementally and in large part through practice initiatives.

During the 1980s the probation service was said to be taking centre stage within the criminal justice process. Community service is very much part of that central role. But there is also a broader and perhaps, over the longer term, more secure role for the probation service that addresses crime within the community. Community service could, once again, be a springboard for the reflective action required of a new generation of probation practitioners.

NOTES

1 This essay mostly refers to the situation in England and Wales, but the significant location of probation within local government in Scotland is mentioned below. Community service orders were introduced into Scotland in 1977, four years behind England and Wales. See especially Gill McIvor (1992).

2 See eg Harding (1974).

3 Interestingly, the term 'building bridges' is not to be found in the report of the Advisory Committee. The report said this: 'But in general the proposition

that some offenders should be required to undertake community service should appeal to adherents of different varieties of penal philosophy. To some, it would be simply a more constructive and cheaper alternative to short sentences of imprisonment; by others it would be seen as introducing into the penal system a new dimension with an emphasis on reparation to the community; others again would regard it as a means of giving effect to the old adage that the punishment should fit the crime; while still others would stress the value of bringing offenders into close tough with those members of the community who are most in need of help and support'. (Advisory Council on the Penal System, 1970, para 33). A few years later Barbara Wootton commented: 'Although the ACPS Report made it clear that the Council emphasised the constructive aspects of the sentence and the hope that it would develop attitudes of social responsibility, we did include a paragraph in the Report of which I have always been slightly ashamed, as an undisguised attempt to curry favour with everybody'. (Wootton 1978, p 128).

4 Recent evidence of the fragility of reparation schemes is to be found in the absorption of the Northamptonshire Adult Reparation Scheme (the majority of the Bureau staff were probation service appointees) into the County Social Services Department. This was the result of the onset of cash limits imposed upon the probation service (Northamptonshire County Council 1993, p5).

5 See Advisory Council on the Penal System (1970, para 61).

REFERENCES

Advisory Council on the Penal System (1970) *Non-Custodial and Semi-Custodial Penalties,* (London, HMSO)

Ashworth, Andrew (1992) *Sentencing and Criminal Justice,* (London, Weidenfeld and Nicholson)

Garland, David (1989), 'Critical Reflections on Punishment, Custody and the Community' in Huw Rees and Eryl Hall Williams (eds) *Punishment, Custody and the Community. Reflections and Comments on the Green Paper* (London, London School of Economics and Political Science, pp 4 to 18)

Harding, John (1974), 'The Development of Community Service: its application and relevance to the Criminal Justice System' in Norman Tutt (ed) *Alternative Strategies for Coping with Crime* (Oxford, Basil Blackwell and London, Martin Robertson pp 164 to 85)

Harding, John (1987), 'Reparation: the background, rationale, and relevance to criminal justice' in John Harding (ed) *Probation and the Community. A Practice and Policy Reader* (London, Tavistock pp 194 to 208)

Home Office (1988) *Punishment, Custody and the Community* (London, HMSO, Cm 424)

Hood, Roger (1974) 'Criminology and Penal Change. A case Study of the Nature and Impact of some recent Advice to Governments' in Roger Hood (ed) *Crime, Criminology and Public Policy, Essays in Honour of Sir Leon Radzinowicz* (London, Heinemann, pp 375 to 417)

Mathieson, David (1992), 'The Probation Service' in Eric Stockdale and Silvia Casale (eds) *Criminal Justice under Stress* (London, Blackstone Press, pp 142 to 159)

McIvor, Gill (1992) *Sentenced to Serve: The Operation and Impact of Community Service by Offenders* (Aldershot, Avebury)

Northamptonshire County Council (1993) *Northamptonshire Adult Reparation Bureau Seven Year Review* 1986 to 1993

Philips, Melanie (1993) *The Observer* (20 June)

Rock, Paul (1990) *Helping Victims of Crime, The Home Office and the Rise of Victim Support in England and Wales* (Oxford, Oxford University Press)

Rutherford, Andrew (1993) *Criminal Justice and the Pursuit of Decency* (Oxford, Oxford University Press)

I am most grateful to David Mathieson, John Harding and Sue Wade with whom I discussed issues arising in this essay: Andrew Rutherford

Endpiece

Collaborating on a book such as this is like starting a jig-saw puzzle, knowing that all the pieces are not available. Any history of community service which aimed for completeness would be an enormous undertaking—and would the picture be much improved? We have aimed to provide a recognisable picture without exhaustive detail because looking forward is now as important as looking back. Nevertheless, acknowledging—and celebrating—two decades of quite astonishing success in community service by offenders was our own starting point. It also provides the launching pad for the wider, more confident use of community service which has been apparent since the implementation of the Criminal Justice Act 1991.

During the last 20 years, community service has become an integral part of the probation operation. Within the wider context of the criminal justice system it has often been the interface between new policy directions from the centre and developments in local practice. The first National Standards produced were for community service and periodically it has been seen as a 'front runner' for privatisation. Around community service, therefore, swirl a number of critical issues, the resolution of which could have profound implications for public service development generally and the future shape of the probation service in particular.

The main thrust of Government policy on public services over the past decade and more has been the drive for improved efficiency and effectiveness. This has been accompanied by what has often appeared to be an uncritical belief in the appropriateness of transposing private sector management practices into public services. Indeed the cutting edge for these changes came from the licence which the Thatcher administration gave to the industrialist Sir Derek Raynor (whose background was with Marks & Spencer).

In considering whether public and private sector are one and the same, Stewart and Ransom [1] have proposed a continuum from generic to differentialist. A generic view makes no distinction between the two whereas differentialists underline unique characteristics of public sector management. These include the pervasiveness of the political dimension, the complexity of stakeholder interest, the central importance of fairness and probity and above all the requirement to respond to unmet need. Public services, unlike their private counterparts, are not free to move into and out of markets.

The generic/differentialist argument is important in relation to the future of community service. There is a danger that central government departments and local services will polarise around positions which will be unhelpful in the longer term. These might be caricatured respectively as a concern with cost and effectiveness against service delivery and fairness. What seems to us to be needed is the development of a public service management framework which embraces both positions and gives them appropriate value.

We have made no attempt to define a 'best model' for the delivery of community service and indeed part of its strength, which has been apparent from several chapters in the book, is based on the diversity of models, of experience, of experimentation and of approach which different probation areas have adopted. That strength can turn to weakness only if diversity begins to merge into inconsistency and arguments over this point were the background to the introduction of National Standards for community service orders in 1988. The Home Office had clearly decided that the point at which the credibility of the community service order was affected by differing standards of practice had already been reached; National Standards were the chosen solution. The first draft of the community service standards, however, was unwieldy, unworkable and unnecessarily prescriptive and was rightly derided as the product of remote and impractical bureaucrats.

Yet beyond the knee-jerk reaction to the Home Office, which was alternately seen as wielding the big stick and starving probation areas of resources (and sometimes both at the same time) the principle of National Standards was worth developing. A good deal of patient negotiation, especially by Lawrence Frayne, was needed before that first draft became a workable document and the second revision of the standards, which coincided with their introduction into most other areas of probation work, simplified and improved them yet again. Given the remarkably impermanent nature of parts of the Criminal Justice Act 1991, comprehensive National Standards, which came into force at the same time, may yet be the more significant of the two.

Certainly the probation service should reflect that the Home Office role, overall, has been a very positive one. That Department played an essential role in enabling community service to get underway in a more or less orderly fashion; encouraged its expansion (though the method chosen may have been eccentric); initiated research and generally allowed probation areas a lot of freedom in interpreting the legislation and providing a disposal in which courts had—and continue to have—a lot of confidence.

Now that the need for standards has been accepted, probation services have seen the benefits they can bring in marketing community service to courts and to the public. Similarly, ACOP and area services generally, have accepted the need to target resources within a clear framework of accountability.

Standards and unit costs are only part of the equation. Section 95 Criminal Justice Act 1991 and National Standards, quite properly, require probation areas to provide services which are open and free from discrimination. It is extremely unlikely that any private sector organisation would be expected to manage to such a high expectation. For community service this involves fundamental consideration being given to processes of recruitment (sessional posts for example can be an important route into the organisation, so how they are filled is critical); access to and experience on work placements must be carefully arranged and monitored, together with the identification of suitable beneficiaries which genuinely reflect the whole community to which reparation is being made.

Many of these processes need to be designed; they will not just emerge as a result of central direction. This will take time because of the careful work

156

involved with a range of stakeholders including courts, local community groups and staff. The concept of design is an important one, especially as it links with the emerging view that quality is better designed *in* by careful preparation rather than by systems which reject faults at the end of the process. In the commercial world the initial investment in design is seen to lead to a reduction in costs in the longer term.

The challenge for the Home Office therefore is to replace the three Es of economy, efficiency and effectiveness with four—equity, economy, efficiency and effectiveness. The adoption of equity would signal a recognition that there are distinctive features to public service management which in turn would strengthen the working relationships between the centre and local area services.

This is an appropriate time to reflect on that relationship. Privatisation, market testing and an interventive government which rarely leaves anything alone in its search for efficiency and cost- effectiveness may well lead to a move to 'contract out' the community service element of probation work. This book contains some powerful arguments against such a move and indeed the very reasons which led to the choice of the probation service in the first place—a national network, experience of working with offenders, close links with courts—are just as important today. Instead, we think the message which *really* comes across from our contributors is that action is required on several levels:

Politicians and the Home Office need not only to leave well alone, but to recognise that, in a time of high unemployment, less rigid rules on work completion may be needed; and—even in a period of restraint on public spending—a better resourced community service scheme would represent excellent value for money. There should be no inappropriate artificial restraints on an option which manages to combine cheapness (in comparative costs) and substantial benefit to the community.

Sentencers might like to look again at the reasons which inform their choice of sentence, particularly when custody is a likely option. The major hope—that community service orders would have a lasting impact on the use of custody—has yet to be realised and Mark Oldfield's view, in *Chapter 3,* that it has become more of an accompaniment to custody than an alternative indicates just how much more could still be achieved.

Probation services have a number of issues to resolve. At management level, the need for a proper career structure for community service specialist staff becomes more urgent as numbers expand. So, too, does the need to ensure that ethnic minority groups as well as women, have equal access to community service. Until services can demonstrate clearly that this is so, the question marks which currently surround this issue will stay—and community service schemes will be poorer and less effective as a result.

There is further potential for using community service to advance an understanding of public sector management. One of the concepts currently being borrowed uncritically from the private sector is that of 'added value'. This refers to the processes in an organisation which add value to the operation. It is a

157

difficult enough concept to apply in a profit-making organisation but even more so in the public sector.

Although it has been suggested that performance indicators being developed for the probation service as part of its Three Year Plan should concentrate on added value, the early signs are not encouraging and suggest that the predominant concerns are actually administrative. To quote Oscar Wilde, this could leave the probation service open to the criticism of knowing 'the price of everything and the value of nothing'.

Surely community service offers tremendous potential for developing a concept of added value which could have much wider application for the public sector. How, for example, might the service quantify the value of wheelchair shopping, luncheon clubs or environmental improvement schemes in terms of real benefit to the community? At a time when confidence in the criminal justice system is low, could such measures include the goodwill expressed by beneficiaries towards community service workers and the units which supervise and arrange placements? It seems extremely unlikely that Marks & Spencer or Ford Motor Company would either neglect such an opportunity or leave it to local offices to develop. There is a role here for the centre, in partnership with area services, to develop frameworks through pioneering research and analysis.

Finally, there should be a clear link between added value and the promotion of the service through external relations. Many probation services are developing an external relations function in recognition of the importance of promoting their work through the media to the wider public. Community service has many good stories to tell but, as with other aspects of the service's work, it would benefit from more public endorsement by those who have the capacity to *shape* public opinion as well as to reflect it. In developing an agenda for the next 20 years we would hope to see equity incorporated with economy, efficiency and effectiveness as the key drivers of community service, a lead from the centre on applying the concept of added value and the promotion of community service at a national level.

And community service staff themselves? They simply have to go on providing a high quality service to the courts and community, producing astonishing results with the most unpromising material, filling the gaps in community provision for the elderly and the handicapped, restoring England's green and pleasant land and coming up with new and imaginative ways of using offenders' time . . . more or less as they have done for the last 20 years. It is to their unquenchable optimism, hard work and commitment that this book is dedicated. They really have earned it.

David Scott
Dick Whitfield

REFERENCE

(1) Stewart J and Ransom S (1988), *Management in the Public Domain,* Public Money and Management vol 8, nos 1 and 2

Glossary of Terms

ACOP Association of Chief Officers of Probation.

BENEFICIARY The organisation or individual which 'benefits from' the community service work.

BREACH Failure to comply with the conditions of a community service order, such as not reporting for work as instructed and may result in 'breach' proceedings being dealt with at court.

CASH LIMIT The financial sum allocated to the Probation Service and to individual probation areas by the 'cash limit' formula.

CENTRAL COUNCIL OF PROBATION COMMITTEES The national body which represents the interests of the 55 area probation committees in England and Wales. (Now Central Probation Council)

COMBINATION ORDER Section 11 Criminal Justice Act 1991 provides for a community order to be known as a combination order, combining probation and community service. The probation element may be of one to three years' duration and the community service element of 40 to 100 hours. The order is available only for offences punishable with imprisonment and is subject to the general criteria for community sentences set out in section 6 of the Act.

COMMUNITY SERVICE STRUCTURES The main models are centralised and de-centralised. In centralised schemes community service is run relatively independently of other probation service operations, whereas in the devolved model it is one of a range of services.

CRIMINAL JUSTICE ACT 1991 Described by some commentators as the most significant reform of sentencing since 1948 and possibly this century. The principles embodied in the Act were developed during the 1980s. The Act provides that the main consideration in deciding on the type and length of sentence should be the seriousness of the offence for which the offender has been convicted with provision for longer sentences to be imposed in cases of serious, violent or sexual offences if they are needed to protect the public.

Non-custodial sentences are to be treated as sentences of punishment in their own right, not as alternatives to imprisonment.

Some sections of the Act were repealed less that a year after implementation but the main principles on which it was based are said to be unchanged.

MARKET TESTING The process of 'testing the market' with a view to 'contracting out' services instead of providing them from within the organisation.

NAPO National Association of Probation Officers.

NATIONAL STANDARDS In 1992, National Standards for the Supervision of Offenders in the Community were introduced. These built on the first National Standard (on community service orders) introduced in 1989.

The Standards, which are signed by the Minister of State for the Home Office and Parliamentary Under Secretary of State, Welsh Office and Department of Health provide:

—a broad and consistent framework for the effective supervision of offenders in the community;

—an important statement to which sentencers, offenders and the public can look as the basis on which work should operate.

PLACEMENT The work location for community service workers.

PROBATION COMMITTEE The body in each probation area which has overall responsibility for the work of the probation service. At present probation committees are composed of magistrates (who make up the largest single group), co-opted members (who may represent local authority interests or have special expertise or interests) and a representative of the Lord Chancellor's Department, usually a judge.

REVOCATION The termination of an order by the court.

SECTION 95 CRIMINAL JUSTICE ACT 1991 This statutory provision requires the Secretary of State in each year to publish information as considered expedient for the purpose of:

a) enabling persons engaged in the administration of criminal justice to become aware of the financial implications of their decisions; or

b) facilitating the performance of such persons of their duty to avoid discriminating against any persons on the ground of race or sex or any other improper ground.

SENTENCING TARIFF The scale of penalties which is generally available to courts and which are often (but not always) used in ascending order of severity. A 'low tariff' disposal would usually be a discharge or a fine; a "high tariff" penalty a combination order or a period of imprisonment. Most community penalties are perceived as within the middle of the scale, depending on the extent of deprivation of liberty.

STAFFING STRUCTURES The organisation of community service varies between probation areas but the following roles are used frequently:

Sessional supervisor: An employee paid on a sessional, often hourly basis; the role usually involves direct oversight of work groups;

Community service organiser (CSO): Community service organisers arrange the throughput of work, identify placements, liaise with beneficiaries, etc;

Community service officer: In some structures, particularly the larger services, this is a probation officer role which involves overseeing the community service organisers within a local unit;

Senior probation officer (SPO): Senior probation officers are the middle managers usually responsible for a community service area;

Assistant chief probation officer (ACPO): Assistant chief probation officers have a policy and strategy oversight of community service at senior management level, held as a functional or an area responsibility.

Index